Mercury by Giambologna

16th-century priest's necklace

Trader's money bag

Gilded bronze and enamel nightlight

16th-century sewing tools

Venetian goblet

The Annunciation by Leonardo da Vinci

Mortar and pestle

Paintbrushes
made from
animal hair

EYEWITNESS BOOKS

RENAISSANCE

Written by
ANDREW LANGLEY

ALFRED A. KNOPF • NEW YORK

Renaissance
hunting horn

Ornate 16th-
century keys

Ivory jester's
sticks

DK

A DORLING KINDERSLEY BOOK

www.dk.com

Project editor Carey Scott
Art editor Cheryl Telfer
Senior managing editor Linda Martin
Senior managing art editor Julia Harris
Production Kate Oliver
Picture researcher Sean Hunter
DTP designer Andrew O'Brien
Consultant David Herman
Photographer Andy Crawford
Researcher Charlotte Beauchamp

This is a Borzoi Book published by Alfred A. Knopf, Inc.

This Eyewitness™ Book has been conceived by
Dorling Kindersley Limited and Editions Gallimard

First American edition, 1999

www.randomhouse.com/kids

Printed in China
0 9 8 7 6 5 4 3 2 1

Library of Congress Cataloging-in-Publication Data
Langley, Andrew.
Renaissance / Andrew Langley – 1st American edition.
p. cm. – – (Eyewitness Books)
Includes index.
Summary: An overview of the philosophy, inventions, art, government,
religion, and daily life of the Renaissance.

ISBN 0-375-80136-7 (trade)
ISBN 0-375-90136-1 (lib. bdg.)

1. Europe – History – 476–1492 –
Juvenile literature.
2. Renaissance – Juvenile literature.
[1. Renaissance
2. Europe – History – 476–1492.]
II. Title
D117.L36 1999
940.2'1– –dc21
98–49766 CIP AC

Color reproduction by
Colourscan, Singapore

Cameo
pendant

Giambologna's
*Rape of the
Sabine Women*,
carved from a
single block of
stone

16th-century
mirror with
convex glass

Contents

Nativity altarpiece by Giovanni della Robbia

The early Renaissance

By the mid-1400s, the period known as the Middle Ages, which had endured since the fall of the Roman Empire, was gradually drawing to a close and a new age was beginning. Italy was at the center of a period of intense creativity, which we now call the Renaissance, meaning "rebirth." There was a revival of interest in the classical works of Greece and Rome, which inspired a new way of looking at the world. Thinkers turned away from the medieval preoccupation with saving souls and avoiding temptation, and began instead to explore people's individuality and to educate them in their duties to society. This became a movement known as humanism. At the same time, artists celebrated the beauty of the human body in more lifelike paintings and sculptures.

SCRIPT SCRAPER
The scribe held a quill or stylus in his right hand and a scraper tool like this in his left. He used it to sharpen the tip of his quill and to scratch out any mistakes. Still, many errors were made in the copying, which were then repeated, sometimes leading to major inaccuracies.

Handle to hold parchment flat

Lamp containing fat and wick

Nearly all texts were written in Latin

Parchments for cleaning ink spills

Inkwell and stylus

MONASTIC MONOPOLY
During the Middle Ages, books were scarce and precious. Each one was copied out by hand by a professional scribe or a monk. At sloping desks in the monastery's "scriptorium," the monks would painstakingly produce manuscripts of religious texts, beautifully decorated, or illuminated, with colored inks. Much schooling also took place in monasteries, convents, and cathedrals. This concentration of texts and education gave the Catholic Church a great deal of power and reinforced its position at the center of medieval life in Europe.

ART OR CRAFT?
Artists in the early 15th century were regarded simply as craftsmen. Sculptors, like the one shown chiseling a figure on this relief, were members of a crafts union called the stonemasons' guild.

Slits through which arrows were shot

Stonemason measures proportions

DECLINE OF THE CASTLE
The thick walls of Caerphilly Castle in Wales stand stark and forbidding. More than 12,000 medieval castles were built in Britain and France alone. They were massive strongholds designed as fortified bases for soldiers. In the mid-15th century, the development of firearms and explosives powerful enough to destroy the strongest walls brought about the end of the castle's dominance.

Cathars being expelled from the city of Carcassone in France

NO DISSENT
The Catholic Church of the Middle Ages was intolerant of anyone who contradicted its beliefs. People who belonged to extreme sects, like these Cathars, were often tortured, killed, or exiled. After the 1400s, humanist thinkers tried to encourage a more tolerant attitude.

A fanciful portrait (1553) shows Genghis Khan dressed as a Western ruler

CORRIDOR TO THE EAST
Mongol armies from the Asian Steppes, inspired by the great conqueror Genghis Khan, built up a vast empire in the early 13th century. In 1241, the Mongols devastated Hungary and threatened Western Europe. Yet their conquests also made it possible for European traders, including Marco Polo, to visit the Far East, thereby stimulating trade and encouraging explorers to find easier sea routes to the East.

ISLAM'S ADVANCE
For nearly 1,000 years, Constantinople was the capital of Christianity's Eastern (Byzantine) Empire. But in 1453, the Ottoman Turks besieged and captured the city, which became a major capital of the Islamic world. This event, shown above, brought one great profit to the West – the arrival of refugee scholars, who possessed valuable insights into classical Greek language and literature.

Discovering the past

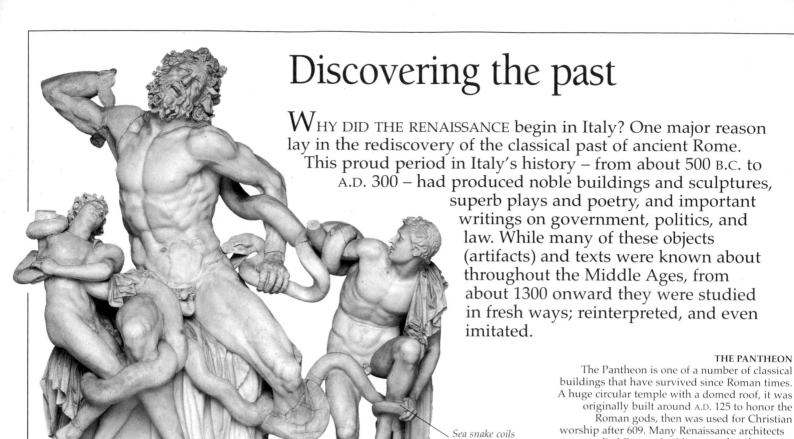

WHY DID THE RENAISSANCE begin in Italy? One major reason lay in the rediscovery of the classical past of ancient Rome. This proud period in Italy's history – from about 500 B.C. to A.D. 300 – had produced noble buildings and sculptures, superb plays and poetry, and important writings on government, politics, and law. While many of these objects (artifacts) and texts were known about throughout the Middle Ages, from about 1300 onward they were studied in fresh ways; reinterpreted, and even imitated.

Sea snake coils itself around boy's ankle

THE PANTHEON
The Pantheon is one of a number of classical buildings that have survived since Roman times. A huge circular temple with a domed roof, it was originally built around A.D. 125 to honor the Roman gods, then was used for Christian worship after 609. Many Renaissance architects studied Roman buildings, so that they could imitate the ways in which classical buildings were constructed. Among them was sculptor and goldsmith turned architect Filippo Brunelleschi (1377–1446), who was particularly thrilled by the Pantheon.

Rectangular portico supported by eight pillars

EPIC INSPIRATION
In 1506, an ancient Greek sculpture known as the *Laocoon* was unearthed near Rome. It was brought to the Vatican by Pope Julius II (1443–1513), one of the great patrons of the Renaissance. Carved in about 30 B.C., it shows a scene from the story of Troy. The priest Laocoon and his sons are crushed by two giant sea snakes, an incident described by the Roman poet Virgil in his epic story *The Aeneid*. This sculpture, with its dramatic representation of emotion, deeply impressed many Italian artists and sculptors, notably Michelangelo (1475–1564).

ANCIENT MASTERS
This frontispiece to Servius's *Commentary on Virgil* was painted by Simone Martini in about 1340. The book belonged to the Italian poet Petrarch (1304–74), who made many neglected Latin texts available, compiled biographies of famous Romans, and even wrote a letter to the long-dead philosopher Cicero.

Latin text

GRACES FROM GREECE

This sculpture, called *The Three Graces*, dates from Greece's Hellenistic period (323–30 B.C.), and depicts three attendants to the goddess Venus. For Italian scholars, the world of ancient Greece was far more remote than that of ancient Rome. However, after the fall of Byzantium in 1453, many Greek scholars took refuge in Italy. Interest in Greek culture grew rapidly, and the Graces became familiar figures in the sculpture and painting of Renaissance Italy.

GRACES FROM FLORENCE

Sandro Botticelli (1445–1510) clearly based the Graces in his painting *Primavera* (Spring) on classical models. The grouping and posture are clear echoes of the original sculpture. Botticelli's Graces also conform with the ancient Roman author Seneca's description of the goddesses as "clad in loosened transparent gowns." The choice of subject reflects the Renaissance fascination with both Greek myths and sculpture.

Loose, transparent gowns, as described by Seneca

Oculus (opening) at the top lights the interior

Span of the dome is an amazing 142 ft (43 m)

Columns supporting the porch and entrance arch

CIRCLE IN A SQUARE

Brunelleschi used classical Roman ideas about proportion and technique in his own projects. His design for the Pazzi Chapel in Florence incorporated the harmony of form he had noted in the Pantheon, based on a circle placed within a square. Work on this small but perfectly balanced building began in about 1430.

THE PLATONIC ACADEMY

Perhaps the most important of rediscovered Greek authors was the philosopher Plato. His thinking had a huge impact on Renaissance thinking. Plato's ideas, and those of his teacher Socrates, were eagerly discussed by the members of an informal assembly called the Academy. They met near Florence at the villa of the influential Medici family.

City-states of Italy

THE ITALY OF THE RENAISSANCE PERIOD, Italy was not a single country. Much of it was split up into small city-states that ruled themselves. As their prosperity grew, the city-states developed their own forms of self-government. Some, such as Florence, were republics where the citizens elected their own leaders and councils. Others, such as Milan, were duchies controlled by a single unelected family. Northern Italy had the biggest and most prosperous cities in Europe. Two growing classes — the craftworkers and merchants — made up most of the population of the cities. The craftworkers produced a large variety of goods, which the merchants then sold all over Europe.

TRAINING A GENIUS
This document records the admission of Leonardo da Vinci (1452–1519) into the Florentine artists' guild at the age of 20. From 1469, Leonardo trained in the workshop of celebrated painter, sculptor, and goldsmith Andrea del Verrocchio (1435–88).

Decoration in enameling and gilt

Latin motto means "Love requires Faith"

VENETIAN GLASS
Venice was famous for its wonderful glassware. This goblet was produced in Murano, the center of the Venetian glass industry. The goblet was a betrothal gift between two powerful families. The betrothed pair are portrayed, one on either side of the glass.

SUMPTUOUS CERAMICS
The first majolica (pottery decorated in bright colors over a glazed white background) was imported into Italy from Spain in about 1450. The style became so popular that workshops for producing majolica sprang up all over the country. The most notable majolica craftsmen worked in the city of Urbino, which, despite its small size, had become an important cultural center. This plate was part of an ornate dinner service commissioned by a wealthy family.

Story of the ancient Greek gods Apollo and Pan is depicted on the plate

MILAN, CITY OF THE SFORZAS
Under the rule of the Visconti family, Milan had been the most powerful and ambitious of Italy's city-states, and Florence's most dangerous enemy. But in 1450, the dukedom passed to Francesco Sforza (1401–66), right, a mercenary soldier who became a strong and peace-loving prince. Francesco's second son, Lodovico (1451–1508), was one of the most powerful figures of Renaissance Italy. He was also a generous patron of the arts.

FERRARA, CULTURAL CENTRE
Ferrara was not large or powerful. But under the Este family, who began a three-century rule in about 1267, this remote agricultural town was transformed into an elegant and stable city-state. Leonello d'Este, (1407–50) right, and his two half-brothers tripled the area of the city, building fine palaces and churches. Due to their encouragement, Ferrara became a thriving cultural center, notable for its music and theater.

CRAFTSMEN CITIZENS
All citizens of Florence could vote or run for office. But to be a citizen one had to be accepted by a guild – one of the trade associations representing the 21 useful professions, or trades. Each guild had its own emblem, such as that of the woolworkers, shown here.

IRON MEN
Milanese smiths produced some of the finest metalwork in Europe, from magnificent suits of armor to delicate keys and locks.

ITALY IN ABOUT 1490
The major independent city-states were grouped in the northern half of the peninsula, which had more fertile farmland and better trade links with the rest of Europe. In the center were the Papal States, ruled from Rome. Most of southern Italy was the separate kingdom of Naples, which was to fall into the hands of Spain in 1504.

URBINO, CITY OF LEARNING
Federigo da Montefeltro (1422–82), duke of Urbino, lost his right eye and part of his nose in a tournament, and so was always portrayed from the left. Though he was an outstanding soldier who served both the papacy and Lorenzo de' Medici as a condottiere (mercenary soldier), the duke is remembered as a humane and learned ruler and a patron of the arts. He deplored the printing of books, and so assembled one of the biggest libraries of handwritten manuscripts in Europe.

FLORENCE THE REPUBLIC
The wealthy banking family of the Medici dominated Florence from the mid-15th century. Lorenzo de' Medici (1449–92) was determined to extend the family's power base. While his first son was destined to inherit his position in Florence, his second son Giovanni (1475–1521) was trained in the Church from the age of eight. Thanks to family influence, he eventually became pope in 1513, adopting the name Leo X.

Renaissance men

IN 1860 JACOB BURCKHARDT, a historian of the Renaissance, referred to Leonardo da Vinci as the "universal man." Leonardo, he argued, had excelled in every branch of study, from painting and sculpture to botany and mathematics. Today he seems the essential example of a Renaissance man – an all-arounder whose talents combined the arts and sciences. But the term means more than this. To a European of the 16th century, the "universal man" was not just a scholar and artist but also a fine swordsman and horseman, a witty talker, a graceful orator, a skilled musician, and a responsible citizen.

A SCULPTOR'S SONNETS
The artist Michelangelo put the same tempestuous energy into his poems that is evident in his sculpture. His poetry often relates his artistic struggles, sometimes humorously. This sonnet, which he wrote in 1511, tells of the physical agonies he endured while painting the ceiling of the Sistine Chapel.

King Henry is pictured dressed in the height of Renaissance finery

EVERY INCH A KING
As a young man, Henry VIII of England had everything. Tall and handsome, he could ride all day, win jousts, speak four languages, play the lute, and talk learnedly about religion and astronomy.

PASSIONATE GENIUS
Michelangelo was one of the most astonishing figures of the Renaissance. He designed tombs, fortifications, and cathedral domes. His sculpture of David was hugely influential. But his masterpiece was the painting of biblical scenes on the ceiling of the Sistine Chapel in Rome.

Silk hose and garter

Michelangelo
(1475–1564)

King Henry VIII
(1491–1547)

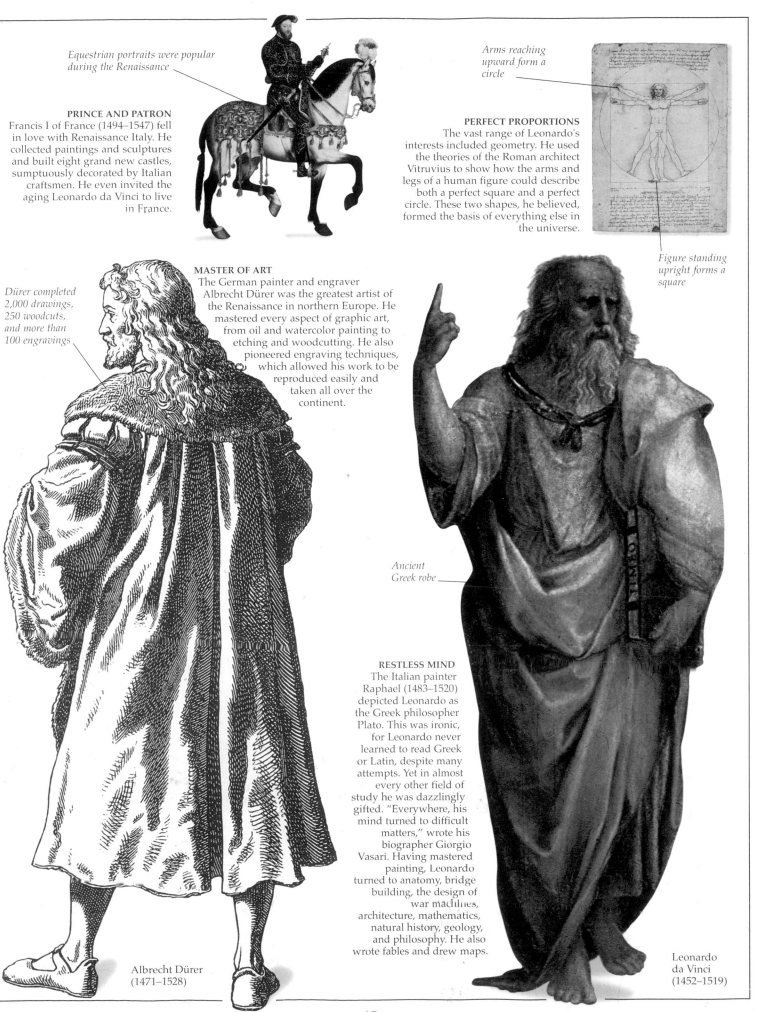

Equestrian portraits were popular during the Renaissance

PRINCE AND PATRON
Francis I of France (1494–1547) fell in love with Renaissance Italy. He collected paintings and sculptures and built eight grand new castles, sumptuously decorated by Italian craftsmen. He even invited the aging Leonardo da Vinci to live in France.

Arms reaching upward form a circle

PERFECT PROPORTIONS
The vast range of Leonardo's interests included geometry. He used the theories of the Roman architect Vitruvius to show how the arms and legs of a human figure could describe both a perfect square and a perfect circle. These two shapes, he believed, formed the basis of everything else in the universe.

Figure standing upright forms a square

Dürer completed 2,000 drawings, 250 woodcuts, and more than 100 engravings

MASTER OF ART
The German painter and engraver Albrecht Dürer was the greatest artist of the Renaissance in northern Europe. He mastered every aspect of graphic art, from oil and watercolor painting to etching and woodcutting. He also pioneered engraving techniques, which allowed his work to be reproduced easily and taken all over the continent.

Ancient Greek robe

RESTLESS MIND
The Italian painter Raphael (1483–1520) depicted Leonardo as the Greek philosopher Plato. This was ironic, for Leonardo never learned to read Greek or Latin, despite many attempts. Yet in almost every other field of study he was dazzlingly gifted. "Everywhere, his mind turned to difficult matters," wrote his biographer Giorgio Vasari. Having mastered painting, Leonardo turned to anatomy, bridge building, the design of war machines, architecture, mathematics, natural history, geology, and philosophy. He also wrote fables and drew maps.

Albrecht Dürer
(1471–1528)

Leonardo da Vinci
(1452–1519)

The new trade

MEDICI EMBLEM
The six balls on the Medici family insignia may represent coins, to show that they were bankers.

By 1460, ITALIAN MERCHANTS were able to offer a wider variety of goods than ever before. There were spices from the Far East, iron and tin from England, leatherwork from Spain, cotton and gold thread from the Levant (Eastern Mediterranean), and woolen cloth from Florence. The demand for such exotic products had grown swiftly during the century as towns became wealthier and society more stable. Traders ventured ever farther in their search for new supplies. From the 1420s, Portuguese sailors pushed steadily down the West African coast until, in 1498, Vasco da Gama rounded the Cape of Good Hope and reached India. Five years earlier, a Spanish expedition led by the explorer Christopher Columbus had crossed the Atlantic and reached the "New World" of America.

Chinese silk

VALIANT VENTURER
Jacques Coeur (1395–1456) was a highly successful French merchant and banker. He became chancellor to King Charles VII and took charge of royal finances. Made a nobleman in 1448, he adopted the motto "To the valiant heart nothing is impossible."

Gap where America ought to be

West African coast

EMPTY OCEAN
The Portuguese reached the Far East by sailing eastward. Columbus set out in 1492 believing that he would reach Japan by traveling west. World maps of the time, such as this globe, showed nothing in the "Western Ocean" between Africa and Asia. The existence of the American continent was unknown in Europe. When Columbus landed in the Bahamas, he was still convinced he was near the East Indies, and searched in vain for gold and spices.

Fugger became known as "Jakob the Rich"

ROYAL BANKERS
The German Jakob Fugger (1459–1525) founded one of the earliest banking firms in Europe. In 1491, the Fugger bank lent the duke of Tyrol (who later became the Emperor Maximilian I) 200,000 florins to finance a war. In return the duke gave the Fuggers exclusive rights to copper and silver mines, which they modernized and made profitable. Like some other businessmen of the time, Fugger employed a fortuneteller to predict the results of his deals.

SILK MILLS
Although luxury goods continued to be imported from the Far East, merchants wanted to produce exotic goods, such as silk cloth, within Europe. Lucca was the first silk-weaving center in Italy, but by 1500 Florence had replaced Lucca as the leader. The mechanical silk-twisting mills of Florence became famous for their fine brocades and velvets.

Cloves

Fine Italian silks

Damask (woven design)

Peppercorns

Cinnamon

ADDED SPICE
Spices had been a great luxury since the Middle Ages. But when Portuguese sailors began to trade directly with India and the Far East, spices became much more widely available in Europe.

COINS OF ITALY
The main city-states of Italy each had their own currencies. But by 1450, the florin had become the most important currency in all of Europe. This small gold coin – no bigger than a fingernail – was stamped with a lily, emblem of the city of Florence.

Coins from Rome

SALESMAN'S KIT
Traveling merchants carried their goods or samples in a bag such as this. Around the outside of the bag are small pockets in which sealed bags of coins were kept. Florins were made of valuable 24-karat gold and were a favorite target of coin clippers, who illegally shaved gold from the edges for their own use.

Florins

Pocket for coins

Memorial fresco by the Florentine painter Paolo Uccello (1396–1475)

IOANNES·ACVTVS·EQVES·BRITANNICVS·DVX·AETATIS·S
VAE·CAVTISSIMVS·ET·REI·MILITARIS·PERITISSIMVS·HABITVS·EST

Governing the people

THROUGHOUT THE MIDDLE AGES, most of Europe consisted of small states that constantly fought with one another. But strong rulers, helped by growing economic prosperity, gradually welded these states together into larger units. By the beginning of the 16th century, the first nation-states had emerged. Among them were France and England, whose parliaments of noblemen passed laws and gathered taxes. Much of Italy, on the other hand, was split between two old rivals – the pope and the emperor. The pope controlled central Italy, while the emperor ruled the Holy Roman Empire (Germany and northern Italy). Both were elected rulers. The self-governing city-states, such as Florence, soon found it hard to keep their independence.

SOLDIER FOR HIRE
Although born in England, Sir John Hawkwood (c. 1320–94) served in Italy as a condottiere, or mercenary soldier. Many city-states employed bands of mercenary troops to protect them or attack their rivals. This left the city's craftsmen and businessmen free to carry on their work during times of war.

A KING'S DIVINE RIGHT
The English king Henry VIII presides over the House of Lords, one of England's two houses of Parliament, in 1523. The bishops sit on the left, the judges in the center, and the noblemen on the right. In England, as in many northern countries, the king's authority was believed to be God-given. However, Henry's decisions had to be approved by his Parliament, and he relied on it to grant him money.

The palace is adorned with painted coats of arms of political parties

Bell tower

PALACE OF POWER
The Palazzo Vecchio (Old Palace) was the center of government in Florence, where the elected councils sat. Completed in about 1310, it boasted the city's tallest tower, from which hung a huge bell to warn the citizens in times of danger, or to summon them for public meetings. The Medici family moved here in 1537, and both Leonardo da Vinci and Michelangelo were commissioned to produce paintings for the interior.

Portrait of Machiavelli by Santi di Tito

PRACTICAL POLITICS

The sarcastic smile of politician and writer Niccolo Machiavelli (1469–1527) reveals his low opinion of human nature. Not surprisingly, his view of politics was gloomy but straightforward: The end justifies the means. His book *The Prince* advised rulers to be as ruthless and deceitful as necessary to bring order and peace to the lives of their corrupt subjects. "It is much safer for a prince to be feared than loved," he wrote.

Savonarola's execution on the Piazza della Signoria by an unknown artist

THE PERFECT STATE

This woodcut is from a book called *Utopia*, written in 1516 by the English statesman Sir Thomas More (1478–1535). *Utopia* describes an ideal society on an island in the New World (America). In this Utopia (the Greek for "nowhere"), all people are equal, all possessions are shared, and all religions are tolerated. More was a deeply religious man who refused to compromise his principles. But English society was not as tolerant as that in the imaginary Utopia, and More was eventually executed for refusing to recognize Henry VIII as head of the English church.

Boat carrying explorers to Utopia

DEATH OF A DOOM MONGER

By the 1490s, Florence's great age was over. The fiery preacher Girolamo Savonarola (1452–98) denounced the greed and corruption of its citizens and prophesied invasion from the north as punishment. In 1494, Charles VIII of France indeed marched into the city. Briefly, Savonarola was the most powerful figure in Florence, but in 1498 he was found guilty of heresy and was hanged and burned.

Later inscription means "Christ is Lord and King"

PRIDE OF LIONS

The Florentines took the lion as their heraldic symbol. From the 13th century, real lions were kept caged in the city center. They were finally removed in the 18th century when people complained of the smell! Stone lions guard the entrance to the Palazzo Vecchio. They flank a Latin inscription that once claimed Jesus Christ as the elected king of Florence, implying that no mortal ruler could have absolute power. The inscription was altered in 1851.

REX REGVM ET DOMINVS DOMINANTIVM

Stone lion is a symbol of the Florentine republic

City of the Medici

IN ABOUT 1466, THE YOUNG LEONARDO moved with his family from Vinci to Florence. The city he entered was vibrant and prosperous. Most of its finest buildings were already completed, but many of the greatest masters of the Italian Renaissance were still at work there. The Medici, a wealthy banking family, were a hugely powerful influence in the city. The modest Cosimo the Elder (1398–1464) was succeeded, briefly, by his son Piero (1416–69), and then by his flamboyant grandson Lorenzo the Magnificent. The Medici not only directed the city's government and policies but also spent vast sums in commissioning paintings, sculptures, and architectural designs from the finest artists available.

The Medusa's gaze was said to turn people to stone

ENEMIES BEWARE
Duke Cosimo de' Medici commissioned Benvenuto Cellini (1500–71) to create this triumphant bronze statue of Perseus in 1545. It shows the mythical hero holding aloft the severed head of the evil Medusa – intended as a warning to Cosimo's enemies. During the casting, Cellini ran out of bronze and had to melt down his own pewter plates and bowls.

Headless body of the Medusa

FIORENZA

VIEW OF A CITY
This is the Florence that Leonardo would have seen as a young man. The painting is based on a woodcut made in about 1470. The River Arno runs through the middle of the city, and medieval walls surround it.

Florence's great cathedral dome

THE MARZOCCO
The lion was the symbol of Florentine power. Statues were set up in towns ruled by the city, and prisoners were once made to kiss the lion's backside. This very human-looking lion, called the *Marzocco*, was carved by Donatello (1386–1466) in 1420, and originally sported a gilded crown.

Shield bearing a lily, the city's emblem

COSMVS · MEDICES · MAGNVS · D · ETRVRIAE

GRAND DUKE COSIMO
Though Florence freed itself briefly from the Medici twice during the Wars of Italy (1494–1512 and 1527–30), the family continued to govern the city's affairs. Cosimo I (1519–74), known as Cosimo the Great, was one of the most successful family members; he became grand duke of Tuscany in 1569.

DEADLY RIVALS
The Medici had many enemies in Florence, including the wealthy Pazzi family, whose emblem showed a pair of dolphins. In 1478, the Pazzi tried to seize power by attacking Lorenzo as he prayed in the cathedral and murdering his brother Giuliano. But the coup failed, and the assassins were executed.

IL MAGNIFICO
Lorenzo de' Medici has become known as "the Magnificent." He was not only a charming leader and generous patron but also a skillful athlete (especially at soccer) and huntsman, a fine poet, and a practical joker.

FINE BINDINGS
Cosimo the Elder and his heirs built up the massive Medici Library, which contained more than 10,000 classical and medieval texts. When the Medici were exiled in 1494, the library was seized by the city council and placed here in the cloisters of the convent of San Marco, which became Europe's first public library.

Arcaded courtyard inside the palace

COSIMO'S PALACE
The Medici Palace, begun in the 1440s, was a grand and imposing building. But Cosimo the Elder found it far from cozy. "Too large a house for so small a family," he said after the death of his second son. He preferred to relax amid the olive groves of his country villas.

ADORING FAMILY
In about 1475, a friend of Piero de' Medici commissioned Sandro Botticelli to paint the *Adoration of the Magi*. This was a conventional subject for the time, showing the Wise Men worshiping the infant Jesus and the Virgin Mary. But, as an exercise in flattery, Botticelli placed portraits of prominent members of the Medici family in his painting – as well as a self-portrait!

Giuliano, Piero's son

Lorenzo as a young man

Cosimo the Elder is shown kneeling before the baby Jesus

Piero, Cosimo the Elder's son

Botticelli himself, glancing toward the painting's viewer

The Church

By about 1500, there was growing unease with abuses within the Church. Many people believed that some Church leaders were more interested in making money than providing spiritual leadership. To raise the cash to support their increasingly lavish lifestyles, they engaged in a number of corrupt practices, including the sale of "indulgences," papers that were believed to grant forgiveness of sins. This unease was to split the Christian world in an upheaval we call the Reformation, which led to the creation of the Protestant church.

WEARING WEALTH
The ostentatious use of the Church's riches was not confined to popes and cardinals. This splendid necklace was probably worn by a Florentine priest. It is made of gilded bronze inset with precious and semiprecious stones, with pictures of the Virgin Mary and baby Jesus in mother-of-pearl.

Sapphire

Dolphin emblem

HUGUENOT SLAUGHTER
By the 1550s, almost half of Europe had become Protestant. In response, the Catholic Church launched its own Counter Reformation to restore Catholic influence. A century of religious wars followed. In France, fear of the growing Huguenot (French Protestant) community prompted a massacre on St. Bartholomew's Day, August 24, 1572, in which more than 3,000 Huguenots were slaughtered by mobs.

HAMMER OF FATE
In 1517, a German monk named Martin Luther (1483–1546) nailed a list of 95 criticisms of the Church to the door of Wittenberg Castle Church. His protests included the infamous sale of indulgences. The Church placed Luther under a ban, but his ideas spread quickly across Germany and throughout Europe, and the historic 95 theses became the spark that lit the Reformation fuse.

CARRY ON, PATRON
Despite religious wars, the Church continued to commission works from great artists. One of the most stupendous was Michelangelo's enormous fresco on the ceiling of the Sistine Chapel in the Vatican, Rome. This detail shows a sibyl (prophetess) from classical Greece.

Removable lid for inserting incense

CENSER STYLE
During Catholic mass, the air was rich with the smoke and sweet smell of incense. It was burned in censers, which altar boys carried to the priest. The practice was adopted from the religions of ancient Greece and Rome.

GLORY IN GLAZE
The patronage of the Church encouraged new artistic techniques. Among these was the use of glazed earthenware, pioneered by sculptor Luca della Robbia (1400–82) in about 1441. For nearly 75 years Luca's formula remained the secret of his family workshop. His great-nephew Giovanni (1469–1529) used this technique to create this ornate Nativity altarpiece in 1521.

BATTLE OF PICTURES
This anti-Catholic medal depicts the pope as Satan. Following the Reformation, Catholics and Protestants waged a war of pamphlets and pictures, with each side portraying the other as evil or at least misled.

Intricate metalwork

Blue was the color of divinity and heaven

Cherub with its hands clasped in prayer

God the Father watches from heaven. The Protestants believed that depicting God in human form was blasphemous

Angels announce the birth of Christ in song

·PVER·NATVS·EST·F·NOBS·

·S·FILIVS·DAI·VS·I·NUIS·

·HOC·OPVS·FECIT·
FIERI PHILIPPVS·
THOME PHILIPPI·
DE PANICHIS ANO DNI·
·M·DXXI·

·HOC·OPVS·FECIT·IOAES·
ANDREE·DE·ROBIIA·A CAP·
SVIT·HOC·IN·TEMPORE·
DIE·VLTIMA·LVLII·
ANO·DNI·M·DXXI·

The new architecture

"WHOEVER WANTS TO BUILD in Italy today," said an Italian writer in the 1490s, "must turn to Florence for architects." At that time Florence boasted some of the most exciting and original buildings in Europe. Most adventurous of all was Brunelleschi's enormous dome for the city cathedral, which was completed in 1436. Spanning 130 ft (39 m), it was the largest domed structure built since the Pantheon was erected in Greece in A.D. 125.

MARVEL IN MARBLE
The church of Santa Maria Novella was built by Dominican monks in the late Middle Ages. In 1456, Leon Battista Alberti (1404–72) was commissioned to complete the stunning black-and-white marble facade. He added most of the upper section, harmonizing with the original design yet incorporating classical ideas of proportion and symmetry. Imaginary lines from the sun symbol to each corner of the base form an equal-sided triangle.

A WHITEWASH
Not all Renaissance work represented an improvement. Originally, the interior walls of Santa Maria Novella were painted with frescoes. But in the 1560s, Giorgio Vasari (1511–74) was hired to modernize the church, and he covered the walls with whitewash. However, the interior's most notable feature can still be seen – the nave piers are spaced closer together at the east end, where the altar sits, to create an illusion of greater length.

LIFTING TACKLE
In the building of the dome, heavy blocks of stone had to be lifted 131 ft (40 m) from the ground. Brunelleschi invented a mechanical hoist, which used ropes running through these pulleys.

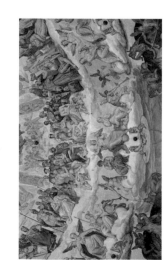

The weight of the lantern helps to stabilize the structure of the entire dome

Globe weighs more than 2 tons

INVENTIVE DESIGNER
Filippo Brunelleschi (1377–1446) was a goldsmith and sculptor before he turned to architecture.

PHILIPPI · BRVNELLESCHI
FLORENTINI · ARCHITECTI
CELEBERRIM · EFFIGIES
OB · AN · SAL · M · CCCCXLIIII

ABOVE THEM ALL
Brunelleschi's dome was said to have inaugurated the Renaissance in Italy, and his fame and influence spread throughout the country.

Dome still towers over the city

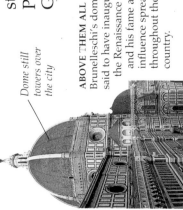

FINISHING TOUCH
The lantern that caps the dome is adorned with a copper globe. It was cast in Andrea del Verrocchio's workshop, where Leonardo was an apprentice, in 1471. The globe was raised up with a special machine that was probably built with Leonardo's help.

DECORATING THE INTERIOR
Brunelleschi planned to have the interior of the dome lined with gilt, while Lorenzo de' Medici wanted to have it covered with a vast mosaic. Eventually, the dome interior was painted with frescoes depicting the Last Judgement.

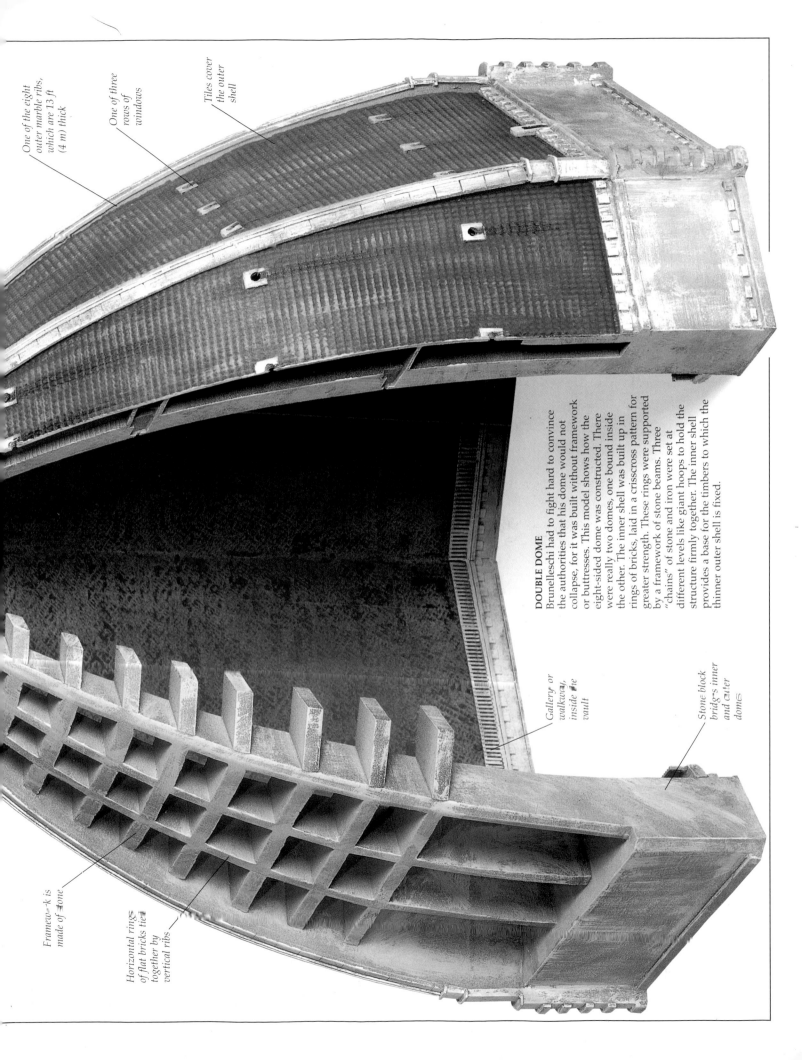

One of the eight outer marble ribs, which are 13 ft (4 m) thick

One of three rows of windows

Tiles cover the outer shell

DOUBLE DOME

Brunelleschi had to fight hard to convince the authorities that his dome would not collapse, for it was built without framework or buttresses. This model shows how the eight-sided dome was constructed. There were really two domes, one bound inside the other. The inner shell was built up in rings of bricks, laid in a crisscross pattern for greater strength. These rings were supported by a framework of stone beams. Three "chains" of stone and iron were set at different levels like giant hoops to hold the structure firmly together. The inner shell provides a base for the timbers to which the thinner outer shell is fixed.

Gallery or walkway, inside the vault

Stone block bridges inner and outer domes

Framework is made of stone

Horizontal rings of flat bricks tied together by vertical ribs

The workshop

EARLY RENAISSANCE ARTISTS were regarded as craftsmen, and their methods of work were strictly controlled by their guilds or trade associations. They learned their trade in busy workshops, which were run by master craftsmen who obtained commissions for them to execute. For the first year an apprentice practiced drawing, then spent several years learning essential tasks such as making brushes, grinding pigments, preparing wood panels, and handling gold leaf.

Quill

Sable brush

Squirrel-fur brushes

MAKING BRUSHES
To make soft-hair brushes, the apprentice tied together bunches of hairs from the tail tips of an ermine, or stoat. This animal is related to the Russian sable, whose fur is used for high-quality brushes nowadays. The apprentice fitted each bunch to a short piece of quill, and inserted a wooden handle. The harder bristle-brushes were made of white pig's bristles, which were softened by whitewashing walls with them before painting.

Mortar and pestle

Mortar and pestle would have been made of hard wood, such as this one, or stone

Hog's-hair brushes

DAILY GRIND
Apprentices had to keep up a steady supply of stock paints. Paints were made by crushing pigments with a mortar and pestle. The resulting powder was then mixed with a binding medium, such as egg yolk for tempera painting, or a slow-drying oil, such as walnut or linseed oil, for oil painting.

Gesso

Bitumen

LADY WITH ERMINE
This portrait by Leonardo shows Cecilia Gallerani (mistress of Lodovico Sforza, duke of Milan) holding a pet ermine with a white winter coat (as used in brushmaking). An ermine was one of Lodovico's emblems, and the animal is also probably intended as a visual pun on Cecilia Gallerani's name – *gale* is the Greek name for an ermine. Leonardo has enlarged the ermine and the woman's hand very slightly to give balance to the overall composition.

GESSO LAYERING
Panels and canvases were covered with layers of gesso, made of a soft mineral called gypsum, before painting or gilding.

UNDERPAINTING
Bitumen brown was used by artists such as Leonardo for underpainting; it helped define light and shade.

The texture of the ermine's fur is rendered in oil paint, using the finest brushwork

PREPARING A PANEL

One of the apprentice's jobs was to prepare wood panels for painting. Poplar, oak (shown here), or silver fir were considered the most suitable woods. First the apprentice boiled the bare wood in water to prevent it from splitting. Next the panel was coated with size, a clear glue made from boiled animal skins. Then it was coated with gesso to give it an even surface for painting.

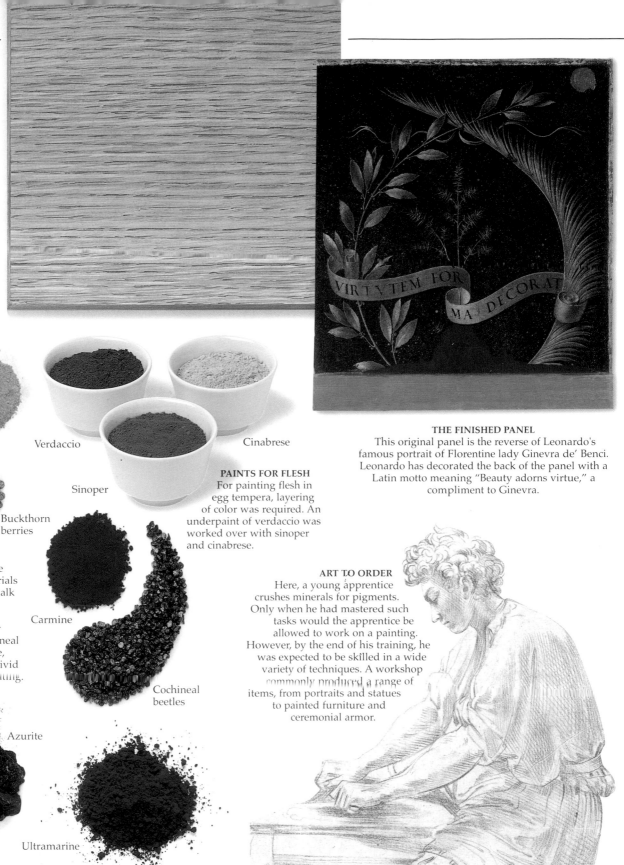

THE FINISHED PANEL
This original panel is the reverse of Leonardo's famous portrait of Florentine lady Ginevra de' Benci. Leonardo has decorated the back of the panel with a Latin motto meaning "Beauty adorns virtue," a compliment to Ginevra.

Yellow lake

Verdaccio

Cinabrese

Sinoper

Buckthorn berries

PAINTS FOR FLESH
For painting flesh in egg tempera, layering of color was required. An underpaint of verdaccio was worked over with sinoper and cinabrese.

BERRIES AND BEETLES

Some colored glazes were made from organic materials mixed with powdered chalk and a binding agent. Buckthorn berries produced a delicate color called yellow lake. Cochineal insects produced carmine, which was made into a vivid crimson glaze for oil painting.

Carmine

Cochineal beetles

ART TO ORDER
Here, a young apprentice crushes minerals for pigments. Only when he had mastered such tasks would the apprentice be allowed to work on a painting. However, by the end of his training, he was expected to be skilled in a wide variety of techniques. A workshop commonly produced a range of items, from portraits and statues to painted furniture and ceremonial armor.

Azurite

Ultramarine

Lapis lazuli

PRICEY PIGMENT

Rich ultramarine blue was widely used in Renaissance painting. To make this pigment, the apprentice ground lapis lazuli, a semiprecious stone, to a powder. *Ultramarine* means "from across the seas," as the pigment had to be shipped from Afghanistan. A cheaper blue pigment could be extracted from azurite.

Making a panel for an altarpiece

CHURCHES OF THE 15TH CENTURY HAD MANY ALTARS, each of which was usually adorned with an altarpiece. The largest and most important altar was the high altar at the end of the nave. This was the focal point of the church. Painted altarpieces might consist of a single large panel or several smaller panels illustrating sacred themes and set in elaborate frames. Some altarpieces were huge, fixed structures that might also incorporate sculptures. Small, transportable altarpieces were sometimes owned by wealthy individuals.

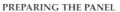

Tool for punching ornament in gold

Charcoal

GLOWING GOLD
The gold leaf of the altarpiece shone out gloriously from the general gloom of the church. An altarpiece was designed to make worshipers gasp in awe at its spiritual splendor; it was also a dramatic way of displaying the wealth and piety of whoever had paid for it – the community, a local patron, or a trade guild.

Ink, for fixing outlines

Egg yolk, for tempera painting

PREPARING THE PANEL
The technique of decorating a panel for an altarpiece is described in detail by Cennino Cennini, a 14th-century Tuscan painter. First, the artist prepared the wooden panel by brushing on a ground made up of layers of white gesso. This was then scraped and polished until it was completely smooth, "like ivory." On this, he drew the design with charcoal. When he was happy with his sketch, he fixed the outlines with a soft brush dipped in diluted black ink.

Unprepared bole

Array of materials used in panel decoration

PREPARING FOR GILDING
Using a stylus, or sharp tool, the artist lightly scored divisions between areas of the work to be gilded and those to be painted. Next, he prepared a special cushioned surface on which to lay the gold leaf. This was made of bole, a kind of soft clay, which was ground, mixed with whisked egg white (called glair), and then brushed on. Layers of the bole mixture were applied to the surface and carefully smoothed with a brush to stop them from cracking.

Boled area is an earthy red and gives the gold a rich, warm color

Gold leaf is so thin that it is difficult to control and can easily blow away in a draft. In Cennini's day, it was handled with a piece of card. Nowadays, a special brush called a gilder's tip is used. To make sure there were no tiny gaps, each piece of gold leaf slightly overlapped the previous one. Only when the gold leaf had been burnished and decorated could the artist begin painting.

Parchment, to stop the gold leaf from blowing away

Diluted bole with brush

Burnisher with agate tip

Gesso ground

Bole

Burnished gold leaf

Unburnished gold leaf

NOT FADE AWAY
Gold leaf was made by beating gold into progressively thinner sheets. It was perfect material for decoration, because it does not rust or tarnish.

BURNISHING AND DECORATING
When gold leaf is first applied, it appears crumpled and matte. To make it shine, the artist needs to burnish it. For this, the artist used a perfectly smooth piece of stone mounted on a stick. The stone might be semiprecious, such as agate, or precious, such as sapphire or emerald. The artist started by gently rubbing the burnisher over the gold, gradually pressing harder until it was burnished to a rich, reflective gleam. The circles of the halos, as in the picture above, were inscribed with dividers or a compass. Further designs might be inscribed with punching tools.

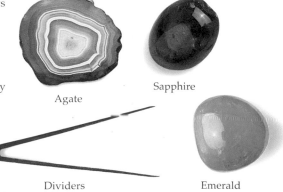

Agate

Sapphire

Dividers

Emerald

PAINTING THE PANEL
This illustration from a French manuscript of 1403 shows a woman painting a panel. Her assistant is grinding up pigments ready to be bound with egg. Until the mid-15th century, artists usually painted panels with egg tempera (powdered pigment mixed with egg yolk), using fine ermine and squirrel hair brushes.

Taming the wilderness

DURING THE 15TH CENTURY, the wealthy families of Italy began spending their summers in the countryside. To escape the noise, overcrowding, and threat of plague in the cities, they built elegant villas in the landscape near Florence, Rome, and Venice. By the mid-16th century, large areas of bare hillside were being transformed into stunning formal gardens, planted with exotic trees and thousands of flowers. At the same time, landscapes and scenes of country life started to become fashionable subjects for paintings. The idea of the country as a retreat from the strain of city life was the beginning of an attitude that is still common among city dwellers today.

GRAND GARDENS
The huge Boboli Gardens in Florence were laid out by the Medici in 1550. The ground was flattened, then planted with firs, cypresses, and laurels in complex geometric patterns. The dip behind the palace was an amphitheater, based on an ancient Roman circus.

IMPROVING ON NATURE
Leonardo was fascinated by the flow of water, and he drew up several projects for altering the course of the Arno River, which flows through Florence. One, shown here, proposed digging three new channels to cut off a bend in the river and improve its flow. In 1503, work was begun to divert the Arno, based on Leonardo's proposals. Although the scheme eventually failed, a modern antiflooding project resembles his original plans.

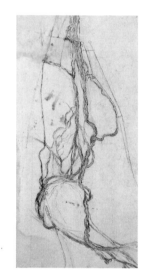

Boats on the river, shown as single lines

THE FIRST LANDSCAPE
The Tuscan countryside of Leonardo's childhood was the subject of his earliest known drawing, dated 1473. The countryside was not yet considered a suitable subject for art, and this has been called "the first landscape drawing in Western art." Every feature of the scene, including trees bending in the wind, is faithfully reproduced.

PALLADIAN VILLA
Architect Andrea Palladio (1508–80) designed the Villa Barbarosa, below, for a rich Venetian family. He based his buildings (most of which are in or around his native city of Vicenza) on classical Greek and Roman models, making use of temple columns and pediments, and emphasizing symmetry and proportion.

Matching wings each contain three groups of three rooms

Classical statues adorn the courtyard

LOVE OF NATURE
Leonardo's notebooks are crammed with studies of animals and plants, such as this red chalk drawing of an oak branch with acorns. He was fascinated by the natural world and felt so tenderly about animals that he would buy caged birds in order to set them free.

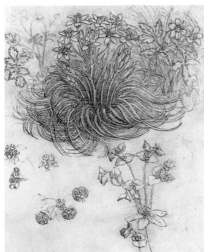

Acorn sprig

QUEST FOR KNOWLEDGE
Unlike medieval artists, Leonardo drew his plants directly from nature. This sketch of a star-of-Bethlehem flower was a study for a larger work. His interest was partly scientific, for he was eager to examine the structures and life systems of plants, and made detailed notes about what he drew.

Star-of-Bethlehem

RUSTIC REALITIES
This 1530 fresco, from an Italian castle, shows grapes being harvested and crushed to make wine. There is no indication of hardship here, although in reality most European peasants lived in extreme poverty. Their harsh lives were often idealized in paintings that decorated the country villas of the rich.

Portico, with pillars and pediment like a Greek temple

Regularly arcaded front walls

Proportion and perspective

THE ARTISTS OF THE RENAISSANCE learned from the ancient Greeks that ideals of beauty and harmony were governed by mathematical principles. For painters, the challenge was perspective — how to represent a three-dimensional image on a flat surface. Brunelleschi showed that if lines are drawn on a two-dimensional surface and made to converge at a "vanishing point," they give the illusion of space and distance. Alberti, Leonardo da Vinci, and others used his theories to explore further the role of geometry and mathematics in art. Sculptors strove to create beautiful and harmonious figures by studying the ideal proportions of the human body. Architects experimented with the principles of symmetry, geometry, and proportion – often with surprising results.

Giambologna's
Mercury viewed
from four angles

AMUSEMENT ARCADE
The principles of
perspective can be used to
create practical jokes. In 1652,
Francesco Borromini (1599–1667)
designed this "perspective arcade"
for a courtyard in Rome. The
arcade is real enough, but much
shallower than it looks – it is only
28 ft (8.5 m) in length. The illusion
of depth is achieved by making
columns and ceiling panels smaller
as they recede. The floor slopes
upwards and its apparently square
patterns are in fact trapezoid.

*Net is placed close
to model for a
foreshortened pose*

DRAWING THE NET
To help him create perspective in his drawings,
Alberti devised a "net." The idea was developed
by the German artist Albrecht Dürer in 1525.
The net was a square network of black threads
stretched on a wooden frame. The artist placed
an eyepiece at a fixed distance from the object he
was drawing. He then looked over the eyepiece
and through the net, and reproduced the outlines
of the model onto a sheet of paper with squares
corresponding to the network on the frame.

Stretched silk threads

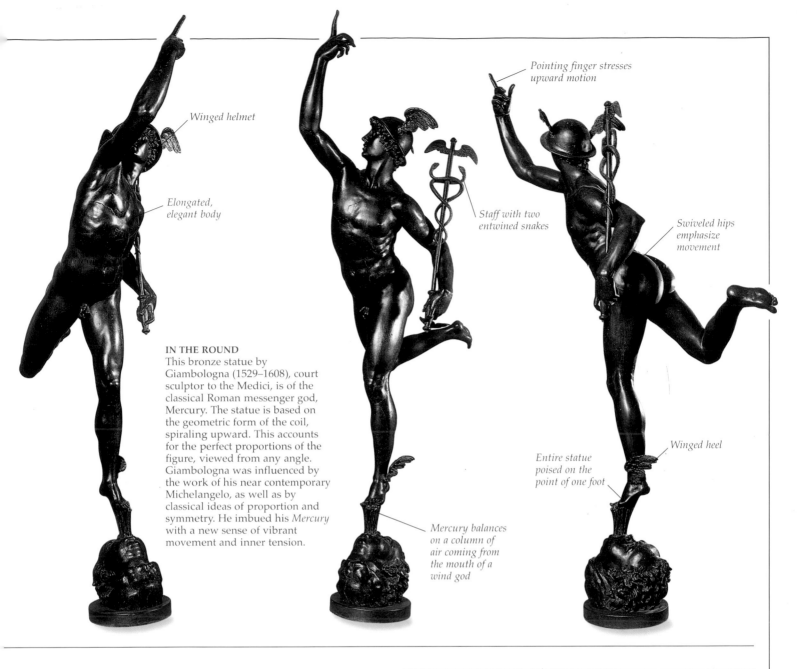

Winged helmet

Elongated, elegant body

Pointing finger stresses upward motion

Staff with two entwined snakes

Swiveled hips emphasize movement

IN THE ROUND
This bronze statue by Giambologna (1529–1608), court sculptor to the Medici, is of the classical Roman messenger god, Mercury. The statue is based on the geometric form of the coil, spiraling upward. This accounts for the perfect proportions of the figure, viewed from any angle. Giambologna was influenced by the work of his near contemporary Michelangelo, as well as by classical ideas of proportion and symmetry. He imbued his *Mercury* with a new sense of vibrant movement and inner tension.

Winged heel

Entire statue poised on the point of one foot

Mercury balances on a column of air coming from the mouth of a wind god

LEONARDO'S *LAST SUPPER*
In about 1495, Leonardo began work on a vast wall mural, *The Last Supper*, for a monastery in Milan, which he had to paint from scaffolding. An eyewitness described how, in spite of this inconvenience, Leonardo would work from dawn to dusk, "never laying down the brush, but continuing to paint without remembering to eat or drink." Unfortunately, the painting started to deteriorate even in Leonardo's lifetime and has since become seriously damaged.

The vanishing point, where the lines converge

POINT OF VIEW
The Last Supper was placed high above eye level. Leonardo made clever use of linear perspective to lift the viewer up to the correct viewpoint. He achieved this by perspective pull – which draws the spectator's eye toward Christ's head.

THE POWER OF PERSPECTIVE
Leonardo's painting is high on the wall of the monk's dining room. Leonardo has painted Christ in slightly larger scale than the disciples, and his head is framed by light from a window behind him. These techniques had the effect of making the monks aware of Christ's presence as they ate at their own table below.

Renaissance rivals

In APRIL 1500, LEONARDO returned to Florence after long years of service in Milan. He was already a celebrated genius, not only in painting but also in engineering. However, he left several embarrassing failures behind him, including an over-ambitious design for an equestrian statue in bronze. Back in Florence, Leonardo encountered another great genius, Michelangelo, who mocked him about the unfinished statue. Leonardo was deeply hurt, and the incident caused a rift between the two. Their rivalry was put to the test in 1504, when both artists were commissioned to produce major murals for the great council hall in the refurbished Palazzo Vecchio. The careers of other great figures of the Renaissance were also marked by rivalry and competition.

BATTLE CRY
Leonardo and Michelangelo were asked to commemorate two recent Florentine military victories – at Anghiari and at Cascina. In 1364 the Pisan army had been defeated by the Florentines at Cascina, and in 1440 the Florentine army had crushed Milanese mercenary troops at Anghiari. For the Anghiari painting, Leonardo studied old records of battles and made preliminary sketches for the characters involved, such as this shouting soldier.

FIGHT FOR THE FLAG
Leonardo's rough sketch for the middle section of the *Battle of Anghiari* shows soldiers fighting to seize the enemy's standard (flag). Here, he is experimenting with the shapes of men and horses under the extreme conditions of battle.

THE CONTRACT
Artists were given contracts by their employers for major commissions. Like this one, the documents usually gave strict instructions about materials and subject matter. There might also be penalty clauses in case the work was late or left incomplete.

RUBENS' RECORD
Alas, neither Leonardo nor Michelangelo finished their commissions. After careful planning, Leonardo started on the central panel of the *Battle of Anghiari*. But he could not resist experimenting. To heighten the brilliance of his colors, he painted onto a surface of plaster coated with a resinous substance called pitch (a recipe copied from the classical writer Pliny). Disastrously, the paint would not dry. Leonardo had a fire lit at the base of the wall, but the colors on the upper part ran, leaving a hopeless mess. Today, there is no trace of the work. The only record is this copy made in 1603 by the Flemish painter Peter Paul Rubens (1577–1640) from a Leonardo engraving.

UNFINISHED MASTERPIECE
Michelangelo started on the cartoon (preparatory drawing for a fresco) for the *Battle of Cascina* late in 1504, while Leonardo was working on his drawing. For once, both great artists were in harmony. In March 1505, the two cartoons were put on display. Then Michelangelo was summoned to Rome by the pope, and he never completed his mural. The cartoon was eventually lost. It was fortunate that Michelangelo's friend Aristotile da Sangallo made this copy in about 1542.

Figure is poised to flee

Aristotile's copy of Michelangelo's figure

FROZEN MOVEMENT
A few of Michelangelo's drawings for the *Battle of Cascina* survive. Like this sketch, they show naked soldiers struggling to respond to the threat of danger. The figures twist and turn, their muscles tense. The Aristotile picture (left) shows how the artist used this particular figure in the cartoon.

Panel shows the sacrifice of Isaac

Ghiberti's winning door panel

Brunelleschi's door panel

Frenzied horse tramples on soldier

COMPETITION PANELS
In 1401, a competition was held in Florence among seven leading artists to decide who should design new doors for the baptistery. The prize was awarded to Lorenzo Ghiberti (1378–1455). Brunelleschi was asked to collaborate with Ghiberti, but he refused, declaring that he would become an architect instead.

Replica doors at the Florence Baptistery are shown below – the originals are kept in a museum

THE GATES OF PARADISE
Ghiberti was to spend much of the rest of his career making two pairs of bronze doors for the Florence baptistery. The east doors (which took 27 years to complete) contain ten panels, each showing Old Testament scenes in relief. Michelangelo called them "the gates of paradise".

Ghiberti's self-portrait in the doorframe

Fashion and finery

DURING THE RENAISSANCE, clothes became even more significant as a sign of wealth and status than they had been in the Middle Ages. Luxury fabrics, such as silks and furs, were widely available. And more importance was attached to dress in Italy than elsewhere in Europe. The wealthy couldn't resist showing off the fine fabrics that their craftsmen produced, as well as extravagant imported materials. Rich families dressed their servants in lavish clothes, too, so that the whole household would give an impression of wealth. Both Venice and Florence passed sumptuary laws, which restricted the wearing of luxurious clothing to specific classes of society. These laws were unpopular and hard to enforce. But in cities without sumptuary laws it was noted that "no difference can be observed between noble and burgher."

HAIR TODAY, GONE TOMORROW
Men's hair fashions changed bewilderingly during the Renaissance. When this picture of an armed warrior was painted, in about 1500, men favored long hair and a clean-shaven chin. By the 1520s, the fashion had switched to short hair plus beards and mostaches. By 1600, hair was long again, but long beards were laughed at.

16th-century ivory comb

Braids, or plaits, twisted to form a figure eight

Raw gum arabic

COMBS AND CURLS
A Renaissance beauty would take great trouble each day to arrange her hair. A wealthy woman would have had an ivory comb, such as the one above, and a special hair-parting instrument. Gum arabic, employed as a glue in the 20th century, was used to make curls stick to the forehead! Thick strands of hair were stiffened with gold lacquer and called "Venus's hair."

Ivory hair-parting instruments

A modern bottle of liquid gum arabic

GIRL WITH DRESSED HAIR
"Among the simple-minded, one single hair out of place means high disgrace," wrote Leonardo. This drawing by his teacher, Andrea del Verrocchio, shows every detail of the model's carefully arranged hair. The most fashionable color for hair was blond, and many women tried to bleach their hair by spending whole days in the sun. False hair, made of white or yellow silk, was also popular, even though it was forbidden by law.

SIMPLE BEAUTY
With her well-balanced features, slightly pointed chin, and heavy eyelids, the face of the *Mona Lisa* represents Leonardo da Vinci's vision of ideal beauty. Unlike the richly ornamented women painted by his contemporaries, she displays no jewelery and wears a simple dress and fine black veil. The *Mona Lisa*'s true identity has never been verified and the meaning of her enigmatic smile continues to be debated.

PEARL BAN
This pendant is decorated with pearl drops. A Sienese sumptuary law forbade women to wear pearls – until the women's protests forced a reversal of the ban.

Cameo depicts the Adoration

Gilt belt, possibly a betrothal gift

LADY OF FASHION
Lavish wealth is displayed in almost every aspect of this portrait of Dona Margarita de Cardona by a follower of the Venetian painter Titian (1477–1576). Her collar is made of fur, and her headdress and necklaces are jeweled with pearls, sapphires, and rubies. Her sleeves are decorated with gold and silver embroidery.

Bead necklace matches bracelets

IDEAL COUPLE
This silver gilt belt buckle was a betrothal gift. While many such gifts are decorated with portraits of the betrothed couple, this one shows an imaginary "ideal" couple.

LITTLE ADULT
This portrait is by Sofonisba Anguissola (c. 1527–1625), one of the first female artists to become famous. It shows a child looking rather uncomfortable in a bulky embroidered tunic and lace ruff. Childhood was not regarded as a separate state from adulthood in Renaissance times, as it is today. Children were thought of as miniature adults and were dressed in tiny versions of adults' clothes.

In the home

THE FAMILY HOME was the center of life in Renaissance Europe. This was partly because the home often doubled up as a workplace. In town, craftsmen and shopkeepers worked in their own houses; in the country, peasants shared their homes with their animals during the winters. Servants and apprentices lived with their employers as family members. Many women died in childbirth; when the widower remarried, more family members joined the home. The husband was expected to rule the household, and his wife to attend to the day-to-day running of the home.

Two-pronged fork for skewering meat

Plain four-pronged fork

Italian Renaissance table forks

Mother-of-pearl handle

FORK LIFT
Table forks were rare in medieval times, when people used knives and fingers to eat. By the early 15th century, forks had been introduced to Italy from Byzantium and the East. Soon, elaborately decorated forks were being used in wealthier homes. However, forks did not catch on in northern Europe until more than a century later.

FAMILY LIFE
Like many other illegitimate boys, Leonardo da Vinci was brought up as a member of his father's household. His earliest home was this simple house at Anchiano, near Vinci. Leonardo's extended family included a succession of stepmothers and sixteen half-brothers and half-sisters.

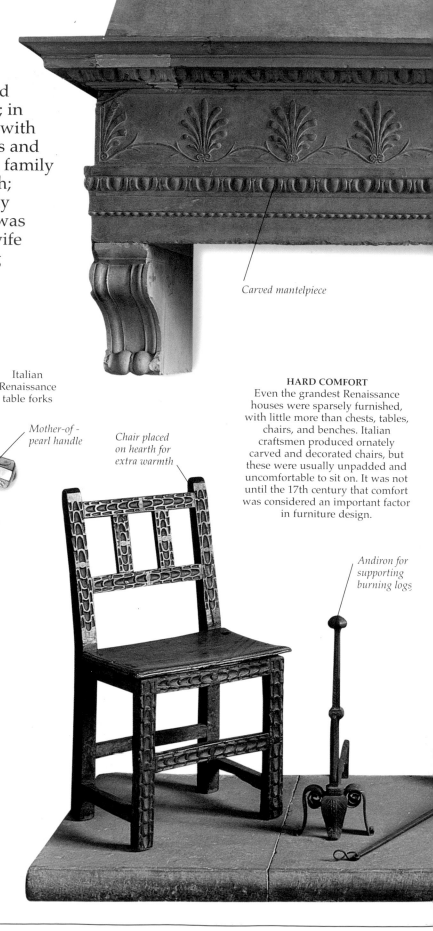

Carved mantelpiece

HARD COMFORT
Even the grandest Renaissance houses were sparsely furnished, with little more than chests, tables, chairs, and benches. Italian craftsmen produced ornately carved and decorated chairs, but these were usually unpadded and uncomfortable to sit on. It was not until the 17th century that comfort was considered an important factor in furniture design.

Chair placed on hearth for extra warmth

Andiron for supporting burning logs

STORAGE POTS

At the beginning of the 15th century, pottery began to be made and valued for decoration as well as for practical use. Prosperous families displayed pretty pieces of pottery, like these storage jars, on their sideboards. The glaze helped preserve the contents.

HEARTH AND HOME

Before the 13th century, fireplaces were positioned in the centre of the room. They were later moved to the walls, and were set on hearths with chimneys to direct the smoke out of the house. By the 16th century, the fireplace had become an important part of a room's decoration, and often had fine engraved or molded mantels. Most cooking was still done over such fires, using either pots suspended from chains, or frying pans with very long handles, which could be placed in the hottest part of the flames.

Chain enabled pot to be raised and lowered

BLOWING A BLAZE

In winter, the fire was covered with ash and left to burn slowly all night. Next morning, it was blown back to life with bellows, such as this Italian pair, carved in walnut, from the 16th century.

Special iron for making Florentine pancakes, eaten with either sugar or cheese. They are still a popular snack in Florence today

A SAFE DRINK

Water in a 16th-century town was rarely clean enough to drink. Most Italians and French preferred wine, which they drank in huge quantities. Even the poorest peasant had a small plot of vines, from which he could make his own wine.

Decorated ceramic jug for wine

Design for living

RENAISSANCE HOMES were more comfortable than drafty medieval halls, but they were relatively sparse by modern standards. Practical, domestic items were frequently inefficient or awkward to use. However, the increase of private patronage encouraged a new awareness of design, and the realization of some improvements – especially for the well-off. Battista Alberti noted that the accumulation of beautiful possessions was a principal preoccupation of family life. Better, and more elaborate, lamps and candleholders gave out more light. Silvered mirrors on the walls reflected the light, as well as the images of those who looked into them. Carved wooden furniture became more elegant, and the development of the mechanical clock meant that time could now be measured more accurately.

PINCH OF SNUFFER
There were only two ways of lighting a room – with oil lamps and candles. Vegetable or mineral oil was burned in small vessels using a fiber wick. Candles were made of tallow (animal fat) or beeswax, which was much more expensive. The candles were extinguished with metal snuffers, such as this elegant pair.

Open fretwork to let out smoke from candle

Intricately carved ivory surrounds the mirror, which is highly ornamental as well as practical

NEW REFLECTIONS
Glass was coarse and discolored until the craftsmen of Venice discovered how to make a clear product, called *cristallo*, in the 1400s. This important advance led to the manufacture of silvered mirrors. For the first time in history, people could see true reflections of themselves. They became more aware of their appearance, and of new fashions in cosmetics, clothes, and hairstyles. Artists also used mirrors to paint self-portraits.

NIGHTLIGHT
In the Middle Ages, most lamps and candleholders were simple in design. From the late 15th century, more decorative lighting systems came into use. In 1490, Leonardo designed an oil lamp with a glass chimney. This gilded bronze and enamel candle container was made in Venice in the 16th century. Its elaborate decoration is typical of later Renaissance design.

Mirrors of this period had convex glass, which is distorting

LETTING IN LIGHT

Until the late 17th century, glassmakers could produce only small panes of flat glass. In a window such as this one, from a 15th-century Florentine palace, the panes were held together with lead. Heavy wooden shutters were used – they kept rooms warm in winter and cool in summer. Such shutters are still used instead of curtains in Italy and other Mediterranean countries. Glass windows and wooden shutters were very expensive, however, and poor people had to make do with drafty oiled paper, parchment, or canvas.

Naturally impure glass is slightly colored

SAVONAROLA CHAIR

In the cramped space of a study or monk's cell, furniture had to be easily stored. This 16th-century chair could be folded and leaned against the wall. It was called a Savonarola chair, after the Florentine monk who used one. The chair was both practical and elegant, with a semi-circular design that originated in ancient Roman times.

Gilded fretwork lid

A SNIP

Large bronze or iron shears were invented in preclassical times. But it was not until the 16th century that small scissors appeared, making tasks such as cutting hair and sewing much easier.

POCKET WATCH

Early clocks, driven by a falling weight kept poor time. In the 16th century, the invention of the coiled spring made it possible to produce much more accurate clocks, as well as portable watches, like this brass one. Such watches were worn on a chain around the neck, as much for decoration as for timekeeping.

DEADLY LOCKETS

These pretty pendants may have contained either a lock of a loved one's hair – or perhaps a dose of poison, intended for any potential enemies.

Curved legs fit inside one another when folded

PLATFORMS

The first platform shoes, called *zoccoli*, were made in 16th-century Venice. These wooden shoes initially had a practical purpose — to keep feet dry in the flooded Venetian streets. But they soon became fashion items. Women were supported by servants as they tottered about on the elevated shoes, which rose as high as 30 in (76 cm). In spite of their impracticality, platform shoes became fashionable again in Europe during the 20th century.

The human body

FOR 1,000 YEARS, the science of the body – anatomy – had remained virtually unchanged. Medieval doctors relied on textbooks and tradition. In the 16th century, a revolution in anatomy took place, led by artists (most notably Leonardo da Vinci and Michelangelo) as well as doctors. This revolution, inspired by the rediscovery of the writings of the great classical physicians, and encouraged by a new spirit of inquiry and observation, changed everything. Both doctors and artists began to dissect bodies and to describe the results with unheard-of accuracy. Consequently, the work of artists and anatomists during the Renaissance is sometimes remarkably similar.

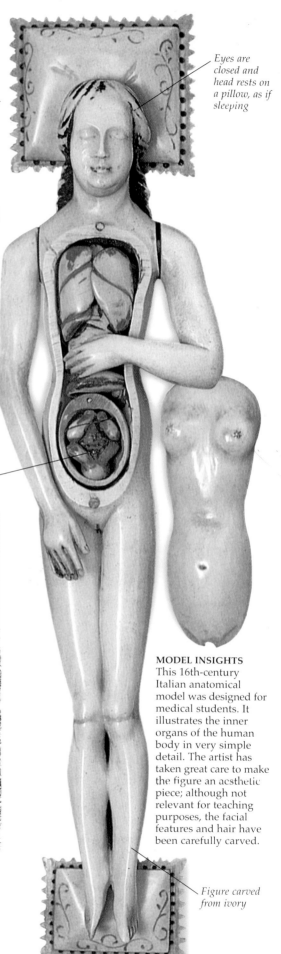

Eyes are closed and head rests on a pillow, as if sleeping

Digestive system

THE PERFECT BODY
Renaissance artists, particularly in Florence, followed the classical example by basing their work on the nude figure. Michelangelo's massive statue *David* uses an intimate knowledge of bone structure, muscles, sinews, and veins to express the body's grace and nobility.

Title page showing a public dissection

ANDREAE VESALII
BRVXELLENSIS, SCHOLAE medicorum Patauinæ profeſſoris, de Humani corporis fabrica Libri ſeptem.

MODEL INSIGHTS
This 16th-century Italian anatomical model was designed for medical students. It illustrates the inner organs of the human body in very simple detail. The artist has taken great care to make the figure an aesthetic piece; although not relevant for teaching purposes, the facial features and hair have been carefully carved.

BATHHOUSE BODIES
Early Renaissance sculptors and painters had limited opportunity for observing the naked human body. The medieval Church discouraged the depiction of nude figures, and most rediscovered classical nudes were in Rome. Not surprisingly, some artists made discreet use of public bathhouses, such as this establishment, which were shared between the sexes.

TEACHING REVOLUTION
De Humani Corporis Fabrica (On the structure of the human body) by the Flemish physician Andreas Vesalius (1514–64) had a profound influence on medicine. Before its publication in 1543, medical students were taught from textbooks written more than a millennium earlier. These texts were not based on the practice of human dissection.

Figure carved from ivory

CUT TO THE HEART

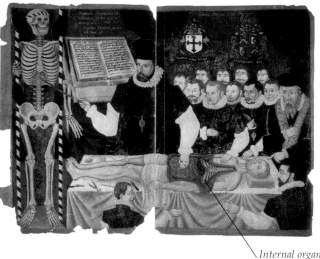

John Bannister, a pioneering British anatomist, is shown here lecturing in London, England, in 1581. Human dissection had been restricted because the Church believed the practice was disrespectful to God. However, by the 16th century restrictions were finally lifted and anatomy became an essential part of a doctor's training.

Internal organs are displayed

Saw, used for amputations

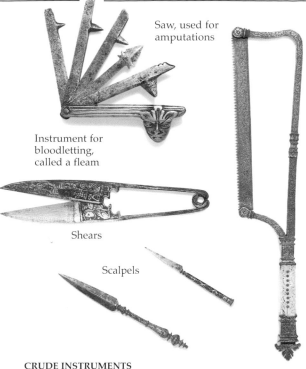

Instrument for bloodletting, called a fleam

Shears

Scalpels

BLOOD AND BONES

Skull made to pivot

This strange, robotlike model was used to teach bonesetting. It was probably designed by the Italian anatomist Hieronymous Fabricius (1537–1619). He also devised operations for correcting spinal deformities and made important discoveries about blood vessels. Fabricius taught with Vesalius at the anatomical school at Padua, Italy's center for the new anatomical science.

CRUDE INSTRUMENTS

Before the 16th century, surgeons were considered little more than mechanics. They had scant training and often doubled as traveling barbers. Their array of instruments was often unsterilized and crude, as above. But the French surgeon Ambroise Paré (1510–90), known as "the father of modern surgery," helped to improve standards. Paré closed wounds by stitching, rather than cauterizing, them.

MORGUE NIGHTS

Leonardo was determined to form a complete picture of how the systems of the human body fit together. To achieve this, he dissected 30 bodies of men and women in the local morgue. The experience of "living through the night hours in the company of these corpses, quartered and flayed and horrible to behold," as he described it, made studies such as this one possible.

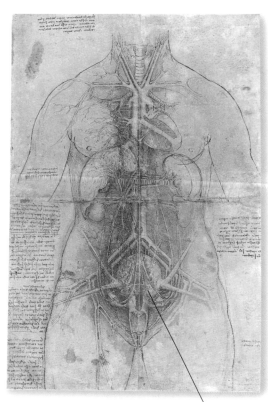

Metal knee joints

Ankle joints

The artist's detailed notes on his observations

TURNING THE ARM

"Human movement may be understood through knowledge of the parts of the body," wrote Leonardo. This study shows the action of the muscles in a man's arm and shoulder. The sequence shows the arms from several slightly different viewpoints.

Uterus (womb)

Dreams of flying

*Flapping
wing spine*

LEONARDO DA VINCI SPENT
much time pondering the
problem of flight. He believed that if
humans could fly like birds, they might create "a
second world of nature." He designed a parachute, using the
shape of a Roman military tent, as well as a form of helicopter. But
from about 1503, he concentrated on the study of bird flight and
attempted to copy their use of flapping wings. Within two years,
he had filled a notebook with sketches and detailed notes. He also
seems to have planned a practical experiment, for he wrote: "The
great bird will take its first flight from Mount Ceceri [near his
home], which will fill the Universe with amazement." It is not
known whether this test flight actually occurred – although there is
a legend that Leonardo's machine took
off, but crashed and broke the leg of
the pilot, who was one of his pupils.

Vertical shaft

*Tilted spiral
screw*

*Leonardo indicated that
the "skin" would be
constructed from cloth*

*The eagle's flight
feathers, used to
produce power and
change direction*

THE FLYING SCREW
Most of Leonardo's experimental ideas about
manned flight were based on the flapping wings
of birds. But, as an alternative, he considered the
principle of the turning spiral screw. He realized
that tilted blades spinning on an upright axis
would create a vertical lift, and he dreamed up a
simple kind of helicopter based on this idea. This
modern model was built from a notebook drawing
of his helicopter, though Leonardo gave no clue as
to how the machine would be powered. However,
his idea anticipated the use of the spinning
propeller, which would eventually drive the first
successful aircraft.

1 OBSERVATION
Though Leonardo was
enthralled by bird flight,
he was able to regard
birds simply as machines.
"A bird is an instrument
working according to
mathematical law," he
wrote. "It lies within the
power of man to make this
instrument." In order to
achieve this, he made a close
examination of the structure
of birds' wings. He noted that
the eagle is a heavy creature, but
its 8-ft (2.5-m) wingspan makes it
supportable. Leonardo noted the
strength and flexibility of the eagle's
wings, and the way they curve slightly
from front to back.

*Secondary feathers form
curve that provides lift*

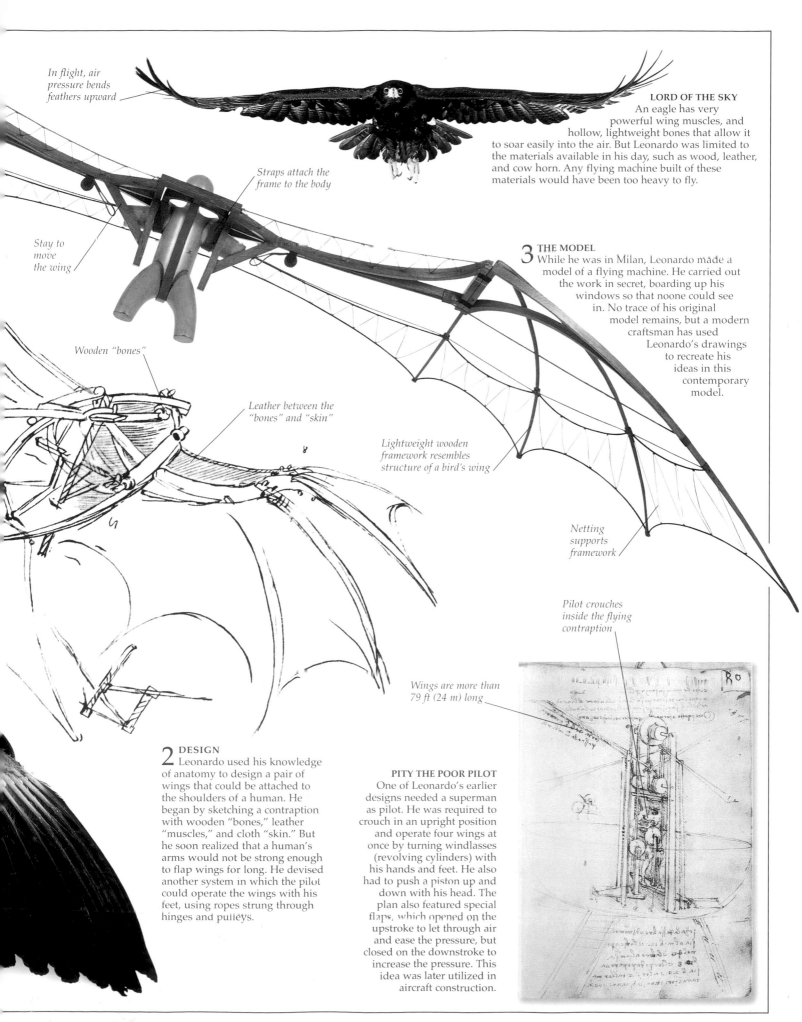

In flight, air pressure bends feathers upward

LORD OF THE SKY
An eagle has very powerful wing muscles, and hollow, lightweight bones that allow it to soar easily into the air. But Leonardo was limited to the materials available in his day, such as wood, leather, and cow horn. Any flying machine built of these materials would have been too heavy to fly.

Straps attach the frame to the body

Stay to move the wing

3 THE MODEL
While he was in Milan, Leonardo made a model of a flying machine. He carried out the work in secret, boarding up his windows so that noone could see in. No trace of his original model remains, but a modern craftsman has used Leonardo's drawings to recreate his ideas in this contemporary model.

Wooden "bones"

Leather between the "bones" and "skin"

Lightweight wooden framework resembles structure of a bird's wing

Netting supports framework

Pilot crouches inside the flying contraption

Wings are more than 79 ft (24 m) long

2 DESIGN
Leonardo used his knowledge of anatomy to design a pair of wings that could be attached to the shoulders of a human. He began by sketching a contraption with wooden "bones," leather "muscles," and cloth "skin." But he soon realized that a human's arms would not be strong enough to flap wings for long. He devised another system in which the pilot could operate the wings with his feet, using ropes strung through hinges and pulleys.

PITY THE POOR PILOT
One of Leonardo's earlier designs needed a superman as pilot. He was required to crouch in an upright position and operate four wings at once by turning windlasses (revolving cylinders) with his hands and feet. He also had to push a piston up and down with his head. The plan also featured special flaps, which opened on the upstroke to let through air and ease the pressure, but closed on the downstroke to increase the pressure. This idea was later utilized in aircraft construction.

Exploring the heavens

THE BASIC SHAPE OF THE UNIVERSE had been defined by the Greek astronomer Ptolemy back in the 2nd century. His theory stated that Earth is a static body at the center of the universe, and that the planets and the sun revolve around it. This geocentric, or Earth-centered, view had become a cornerstone of Western thought – especially religion. But the Renaissance provoked a fresh spirit of inquiry. In 1543, the Polish astronomer Nicolaus Copernicus (1473–1543) put forward an amazing new theory: that the sun is at the center of the universe, around which Earth and the other planets revolve. This idea led to a revolution in astronomy.

MARINER'S MODEL
The armillary sphere had been used since Ptolemy's time to teach navigators and others about the arrangement of the heavens. It was a hollow model of the solar system, with Earth at the center and metal rings representing the paths of the sun and the planets.

Metal rings rotate to show the courses of the planets

HEAVENS ABOVE
Thanks to the development of the telescope, the Italian physicist and astronomer Galileo Galilei (1564–1642) was able to observe the night sky in greater detail than anyone before him. He discovered that several moons revolve around Jupiter. This meant that not all heavenly bodies circled Earth; therefore it could not be at the center of the universe. Copernicus's theory was proved correct.

Venetian senators amazed at the view through Galileo's telescope

TRACKING THE PLANETS
From his observatory near Copenhagen, Denmark, astronomer Tycho Brahe (1546–1601) made precise recordings of the movements of the planets. His observations were so accurate that the first complete modern stellar atlas was produced from them.

THE PTOLEMAIC SYSTEM
Earth sits at the center of Ptolemy's universe, circled by the planets and stars. Christian teaching used this system to show that God had designed the universe for the sole benefit of human beings.

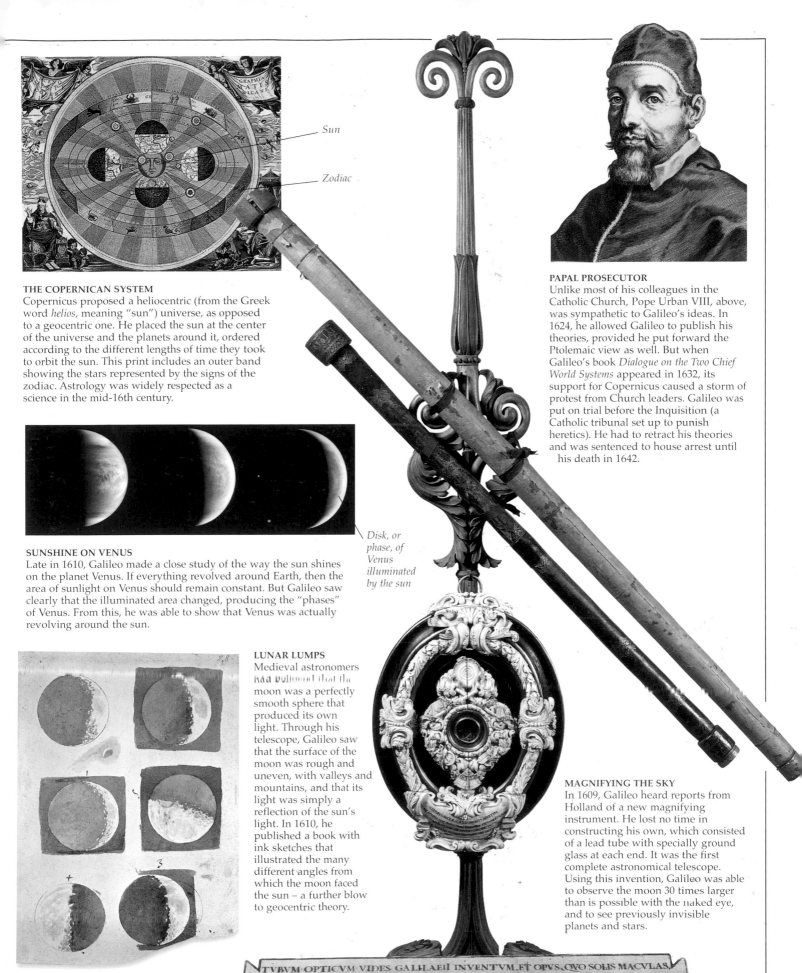

THE COPERNICAN SYSTEM

Copernicus proposed a heliocentric (from the Greek word *helios*, meaning "sun") universe, as opposed to a geocentric one. He placed the sun at the center of the universe and the planets around it, ordered according to the different lengths of time they took to orbit the sun. This print includes an outer band showing the stars represented by the signs of the zodiac. Astrology was widely respected as a science in the mid-16th century.

Sun

Zodiac

SUNSHINE ON VENUS

Late in 1610, Galileo made a close study of the way the sun shines on the planet Venus. If everything revolved around Earth, then the area of sunlight on Venus should remain constant. But Galileo saw clearly that the illuminated area changed, producing the "phases" of Venus. From this, he was able to show that Venus was actually revolving around the sun.

Disk, or phase, of Venus illuminated by the sun

LUNAR LUMPS

Medieval astronomers had believed that the moon was a perfectly smooth sphere that produced its own light. Through his telescope, Galileo saw that the surface of the moon was rough and uneven, with valleys and mountains, and that its light was simply a reflection of the sun's light. In 1610, he published a book with ink sketches that illustrated the many different angles from which the moon faced the sun – a further blow to geocentric theory.

PAPAL PROSECUTOR

Unlike most of his colleagues in the Catholic Church, Pope Urban VIII, above, was sympathetic to Galileo's ideas. In 1624, he allowed Galileo to publish his theories, provided he put forward the Ptolemaic view as well. But when Galileo's book *Dialogue on the Two Chief World Systems* appeared in 1632, its support for Copernicus caused a storm of protest from Church leaders. Galileo was put on trial before the Inquisition (a Catholic tribunal set up to punish heretics). He had to retract his theories and was sentenced to house arrest until his death in 1642.

MAGNIFYING THE SKY

In 1609, Galileo heard reports from Holland of a new magnifying instrument. He lost no time in constructing his own, which consisted of a lead tube with specially ground glass at each end. It was the first complete astronomical telescope. Using this invention, Galileo was able to observe the moon 30 times larger than is possible with the naked eye, and to see previously invisible planets and stars.

TVBVM OPTICVM VIDES GALILAEII INVENTVM, ET OPVS, QVO SOLIS MACVLAS, ET EXTIMOS LVNAE MONTES, ET IOVIS SATELLITES, ET NOVAM QVASI RERVM VNIVERSITATE PRIMVS DISPEXIT A, MDCIX.

Warfare

In the 15th century, Italy was afflicted first by wars between the city-states, and then by a French invasion. In the 16th century, wars over religion divided the whole of Europe. The development of firearms and explosives led to a rapid advance in the technology of warfare. The military engineer became an important figure, not simply for designing weapons, but for improving fortifications, building bridges, and even diverting rivers to destroy the enemy. When Leonardo da Vinci moved to Milan in 1482, he wrote to the duke, Lodovico Sforza, and offered his services as an engineer who could design anything from giant catapults to warships.

CANNONIZED
When the French armies invaded Italy in 1494, the Italians were impressed by their advanced weaponry, which included cannons that fired iron balls. In Florence, the Medici later ordered similar cannons to be made. Some were even decorated with cast heads of saints, such as Saint Peter, above.

Shells explode on impact

MORTAR BOMBS
"I have bombardment devices that will hurl rocks as thickly as hailstones, with the smoke causing great terror to the enemy," wrote Leonardo to Lodovico Sforza. His mortar cannon was designed to lob shells in an arc over defensive walls. The shells would then explode, shattering small stones like modern shrapnel.

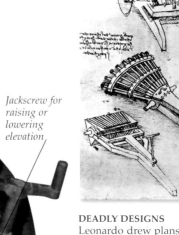

DEADLY DESIGNS
Leonardo drew plans for three different kinds of rapid-fire cannons, above. The top one has all barrels pointing in a single direction, the middle one has splayed barrels, and the bottom one has three racks of guns, which could be fired one after another.

Jackscrew for raising or lowering elevation

Iron-rimmed wheels

SPRAYING THE TARGET
None of Leonardo's multi-barreled guns was built in his lifetime, but this modern model is based on his designs. The eight light cannon could fire iron-tipped bolts over a wide area – a deadly tactic against an advancing body of troops.

Flap gives access for reloading

Wheel-lock gun

Wheel-lock pistol

Butt could be used as a club

Magazine for storing spare flints

LOCK, STOCK, AND BARREL

Gunpowder had been used for warfare in Europe since the 14th century, but it was only after about 1425 that small arms became effective in battle. Both the wheel-lock gun and pistol, above, are from the late 1500s and are operated by the same mechanism. They were fired by pulling a trigger that spun a wheel. The wheel struck sparks from a flint or piece of iron pyrites, and the sparks ignited the gunpowder. Despite their power, such weapons were expensive to make and slow to reload.

POWDER FLASK

Soldiers carried flasks filled with gunpowder, which they tipped out of the spout when reloading their weapons. The flasks were made of nonferrous materials, such as horn, to prevent accidental sparks.

Lion's head, a symbol of Florence

MEDICI SWORD

Swords were still vital weapons in 16th-century warfare, and Milanese ironworkers were famed throughout Europe for the high quality and beauty of their arms and armor. This ornate falchion, or short cutting sword, is engraved with the crest of Cosimo I de' Medici.

Medici coat of arms

PROUD SOLDIER

Leonardo's drawing of a warrior conveys all the arrogance and cruelty of the condottieri, or mercenary soldiers, hired by several of the city-states to fight their battles. By 1509, Venice employed nearly 30,000 of them. In fact, some mercenary bands prolonged wars so that they could continue to receive their wages.

Death and disease

BETWEEN THE 10TH AND 15TH CENTURIES, diseases such as smallpox, dysentery, and typhus arrived in Europe, brought by travelers from other countries. Most virulent of all was the plague, which reached Italy in 1348. Florence, like many other cities, lost more than one third of its population. Further outbreaks of the plague continued throughout the 15th and 16th centuries. Contact with the New World (the Americas) was the probable cause of the introduction of syphilis, which spread across Europe in the 1490s. Treatment of disease was often based on superstition and prayer. Meanwhile, death in childbirth, high infant mortality, and constant warring continued to make Renaissance Europe a dangerous place to live.

SEARING PAIN
The cautery iron was heated until red-hot and applied to wounds and ulcers. It seared the flesh and stopped bleeding, destroying the swellings caused by the plague but not the infection itself.

PRIEST'S PROTECTOR
Priests were often called to bless the sick and dying. To protect themselves from infection, they used a long-handled instrument like this for offering communion bread and wine, and for sprinkling holy water on the patient.

BLOODSUCKERS
Doctors believed that many illnesses could be relieved by draining "poisons" or excess blood from the body – a process known as bloodletting. Some used medicinal leeches to suck out blood.

DUTY TO THE SICK
This manuscript illumination shows an Italian hospital of the 15th century. Care of the sick was considered a religious duty, and wealthy merchants gave money to found hospitals. On a visit to Italy in 1511, Martin Luther noted that "the hospitals are handsomely built and admirably provided with careful attendants." However, treatment was mostly ineffectual, and victims of disease were encouraged to concentrate on the fate of their souls rather than that of their bodies.

CARRYING THE PLAGUE
The plague was first brought to Italy in ships returning from the Black Sea. The virus was carried by a species of flea that lived on black rats and other rodents. Once on dry land, the rats lived in people's homes and spread the deadly virus to humans.

Plague fleas infested the fur of the rat

CROSSES OF LEAD
Without any cure for the plague, people took preventive measures, which could be cruel as well as sensible. Infected families were boarded up in their houses, patients were isolated in plague hospitals, infected clothing was burned, and bodies were buried in mass graves, or plague pits, well away from the towns. Coffins were scarce, so a simple lead cross was placed on each corpse.

Cautery iron

Communion instrument

DEATH TAKES A CHILD
This woodcut shows a child being dragged from his parents by a devil (representing death). Repeated outbreaks of the plague reinforced the medieval belief that illness and early death were punishments from God for human wickedness. Such beliefs were particularly strong in northern Europe.

Map showing the signs of the zodiac

SYPHILITIC STARS
Syphilis caused sores and pustules to form all over the victim's body. Albrecht Dürer depicted the harrowing consequences of the disease in this woodcut, which also illustrates the power of superstition. The globe above the victim's head displays the year 1484, when a new outbreak of plague was thought to have been caused by the appearance of five planets in the zodiacal sign of the scorpion.

POISONOUS CURE
In 1512, doctors began to use mercury to treat syphilis. They did not realize that mercury is poisonous and can be deadly.

Crib decorated with mythological figures

DEATH AT BIRTH
In Renaissance Europe, between a quarter and a half of all babies died in their first year. With little proper treatment available, common illnesses such as influenza and measles easily killed vulnerable babies. Children born to poor families were also particularly at risk from malnutrition.

16th-century Italian baby's crib

A reading public

THE INVENTION OF THE PRINTING PRESS was one of the most dramatic developments to affect the Renaissance world. Printing had first been developed in China, where movable type was used as early as the 11th century. But it was not until the 1450s that the method was adopted in Europe, when the German Johannes Gutenberg (c. 1398–1468) began printing entire books using movable type cast in metal. For the first time, exact copies of books could be produced quickly and cheaply. By about 1500 there were more than 1,000 printing workshops in Europe, mostly in Germany and Italy.

IN THE WORKSHOP
The bustle of a printing office was very different from the quiet of a medieval scribe's desk. This 16th-century picture shows everyone hard at work. The compositor sets type, the printers operate the press, and the proofreader checks a printed page for errors. Only the dog is asleep.

Q_uæ postquam uates_

ITALIAN ITALICS
German printers used thick, Gothic type that resembled that of old manuscripts. Italian printers cast smaller types, such as *italic*, shown above, and roman. With these typefaces, more words could fit on a page, so fewer pages were needed, and books became smaller and cheaper.

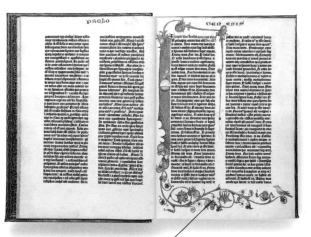

Printed books continued to be decorated by hand

GUTENBERG BIBLE
Gutenberg was a skilled craftsman. He built his printing press by applying the principle of the press used to crush grapes for wine, and he engraved metal punches for molding the type in relief. His workshop could print about 300 sheets each day. In 1455, Gutenberg produced his first complete printed book – the Bible. His edition, known as the Gutenberg Bible, contained more than 1,200 pages in two volumes, and it probably took several years to set and print.

PROUD PRINTER
Johannes Gutenberg displays a newly printed sheet in his workshop.

Pieces of type specially shaped to fit neatly together

TYPESETTING
Each character, or letter, was cast (in mirror image) on a separate piece of type. The compositor picked out the type and set it in order on a "stick," left. Spaces between words or blocks of text were filled with blank "leading." The movable grip on the left fixed the line length.

Grip

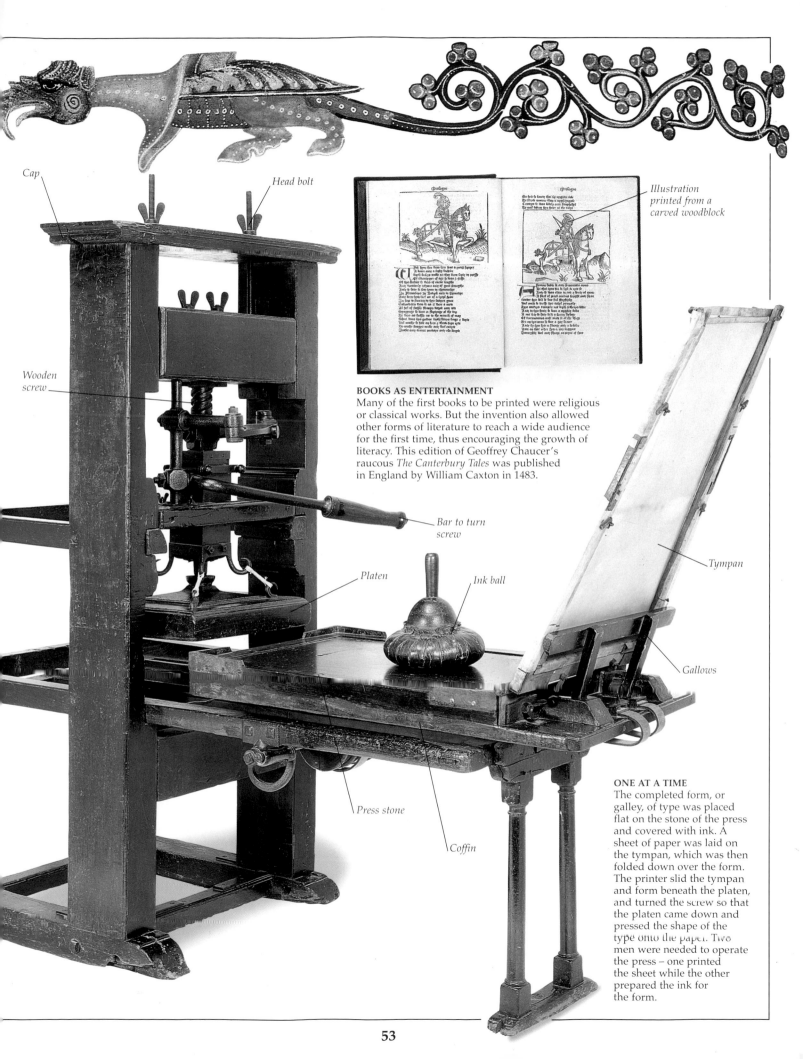

Cap

Head bolt

Illustration printed from a carved woodblock

Wooden screw

BOOKS AS ENTERTAINMENT
Many of the first books to be printed were religious or classical works. But the invention also allowed other forms of literature to reach a wide audience for the first time, thus encouraging the growth of literacy. This edition of Geoffrey Chaucer's raucous *The Canterbury Tales* was published in England by William Caxton in 1483.

Bar to turn screw

Platen

Ink ball

Tympan

Gallows

Press stone

Coffin

ONE AT A TIME
The completed form, or galley, of type was placed flat on the stone of the press and covered with ink. A sheet of paper was laid on the tympan, which was then folded down over the form. The printer slid the tympan and form beneath the platen, and turned the screw so that the platen came down and pressed the shape of the type onto the paper. Two men were needed to operate the press – one printed the sheet while the other prepared the ink for the form.

Music and leisure

WORKING LIFE WAS HARD for most people in Renaissance Europe, and there was little money or time to spend on entertainment. But even the poorest could enjoy the regular religious feast days, which meant a day's holiday from work, free food, and the excitement of processions, horse races, and mock battles. The people could also go to the great churches to hear the pure, sensuous new music for the Mass. The wealthy, of course, could afford far grander amusements, including many outdoor sports, especially hunting.

COMPOSER FOR THE CHURCH
Giovanni Pierluigi da Palestrina (c. 1525–94) composed more than 100 settings of the Mass and many simpler works for unaccompanied voices. His choral compositions were intricate and sumptuous, while the words were always clear and intelligible.

NOTES ON THE PAGE
The invention of printing had a huge impact on music. For the first time, scores could be copied accurately and quickly, and they were sold widely throughout Europe. The first music printed from movable type was published by Ottaviano Petrucci in Venice in 1501. He went on to produce more than 59 volumes, from polyphony to lute music, shown above.

LEONARDO'S MUSIC
Leonardo had a fine singing voice and was a skilled player of the lira da braccia (left). He made his own lyre from silver, which was said to have a more resonant and beautiful sound than a conventional wooden lyre. His notebooks also contain studies for many other instruments, including mechanical drums and wind instruments with keyboards. For Leonardo, music was "the representation of invisible things" and the sister of painting.

An angel plays heavenly music on the lute

Music

Renaissance music was written mainly for voices. The great choirs of the cathedrals sang settings of the liturgy (religious services) or oratorios (religious stories set to music). The style was polyphonic, which means it contained several melodies that were sung simultaneously. Outside the church, the most popular form of music was the madrigal, which was usually romantic poetry with parts for several voices.

Hunting

Hunting had been a popular pastime for the wealthy and nobility since the Middle Ages, and its popularity continued in Renaissance times. Hunting parties could be enormous – entire courts might take part – and could last for several weeks. It was also highly energetic; it was said that Henry VIII of England could wear out eight horses in a single day's hunting.

HAWK HOOD
Birds and small animals were hunted with falcons. The falconer placed a hood, such as this one, over the falcon's head in order to "hoodwink" it into thinking it was night, so the bird would remain calm. When the hunter spotted suitable game, he removed the hood and released his hawk.

Decorative feather plume

HUNTING HORN
The huntsman organized the hunt and led the hounds. He blew a horn to signal that game was sighted, or to indicate the direction in which it was headed. Some hunting horns were very ornate, such as this one made of buffalo horn and gilded bronze.

A WOMAN'S WEAPON
This unusual crossbow was made especially for a woman. Designed for shooting birds, it used clay balls instead of arrows. Although most hunters were men, some women, including Queen Elizabeth I of England (1533–1603), also enjoyed the sport.

Trigger for releasing bowstring

Festivals

Leisure time was associated not with weekends, as it is now, but with public holidays (holy days), which were much more numerous than they are today. Holidays were festival days, celebrated with plays, games, and processions.

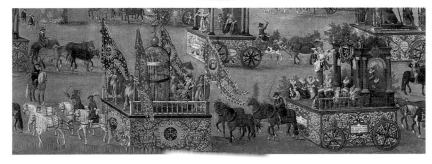

THE OMMEGANCK PROCESSION
Royal processions were also occasions for festivals. In 1615, the townsfolk of Brussels, Belgium, were treated to a particularly spectacular triumphal procession celebrating the entry of the regent Isabella. It featured more than a dozen floats carrying people dressed as symbolic and mythical figures.

Face embossed in metal

HELMETS ON PARADE
This Italian casque, or open helmet, was made in about 1530, especially for use in parades. Such helmets were worn for carnival, the wildest of all Italian festivals, celebrated during the period preceding Lent. In addition to parades, it included huge banquets, organized races, and tournaments.

RENAISSANCE REVISITED
The parades of medieval and Renaissance times are still reenacted. At this festival in Oristano, Sardinia, a procession of drummers, trumpeters, and knights parades through the city. Held each February, the festival is thought to bring a prosperous year.

The Renaissance in the north

"IMMORTAL GOD, what a world I see dawning!," wrote the Dutch humanist Erasmus in 1517. Like other northern scholars and scientists, he was thrilled by the new horizons opened up by the Renaissance in Italy. Artists such as Dürer and Holbein, too were inspired by Italian masters. Many traveled to Italy to study the rediscovered classical texts, absorb new ideas, and acquire new techniques. At the same time, patrons such as Francis I of France encouraged Italian artists, and promoted the use of printed books and manuscripts.

HONEST ESSAYIST
"I myself am the subject of my book," admitted Michel de Montaigne (1533–92) in the introduction to his essays, written in a secluded tower in France. No writer before had ever revealed himself so honestly or humanely. Montaigne's thoughts on friendship, parenthood, and other personal matters exemplify the spirit of Renaissance humanism.

Tiny, distant figures skate on the ice

FROZEN LANDSCAPE
The Flemish artist Pieter Breughel the Elder (c. 1525–69) traveled from Flanders to Italy, although he was more inspired by the Alps than by Italian art. His detailed landscapes, such as this one, *Hunters in the Snow* (1565), show country people in their natural environment. His work illustrates the lively realism of much northern painting.

IDEAL BEAUTY
Painted by Albrecht Dürer in 1507, these twin pictures of Adam and Eve are the first idealized nudes in German art. They embody the classical quest for ideal beauty that was common to Italian art. Dürer was responsible for bringing many Italian Renaissance ideas to northern Europe.

JOURNEY TO THE UNDERWORLD
Flemish painter Joachim Patinir (c. 1480–1525) has been referred to as the first Western artist known to have specialized in landscape painting. The subject of *Crossing the River Styx* is a mythological one – the souls of the dead are being rowed across the river to the Underworld by Charon, the ferryman. Patinir combined a strong sense of fantasy with a brilliant use of light and shade and detailed observation.

DUTCH SCHOLAR

Desiderius Erasmus (1466–1536) traveled widely throughout Europe. A leading humanist scholar of the northern Renaissance, he succeeded in popularizing a range of classical texts for ordinary readers. He also attacked corruption in the Catholic Church, although he did not support the Protestant movement. This portrait was painted by his friend, the German artist Hans Holbein (1497–1543), who is famous for his realistic depictions of physical features.

NUREMBERG, CITY OF CULTURE

By the mid-16th century, Nuremberg, in southern Germany, had become a prosperous trading and cultural center. The city was home to important artists such as Dürer, and it boasted one of the first printing presses and a library containing 4,000 volumes. Printmakers, mapmakers, and astronomers, as well as artists and scholars, were attracted to Nuremberg by wealthy patrons.

A candle burning in a daylit room was traditional for newlyweds

Dog symbolizes obedience

GARGANTUAN SUCCESS

French writer François Rabelais (c. 1490–1553) ridiculed old-fashioned, formal ways of teaching compared to the new humanism in his boisterous, comic novels *Pantagruel* (1532), and *Gargantua* (1534). They were massive best sellers throughout Europe, although they were banned in France for some time.

DOMESTIC DETAILS

Artists in the Netherlands pioneered their own oil-painting techniques in the early 15th century, creating a naturalistic style that influenced even Italian painters. Jan van Eyck (c. 1390–1441) painted this double portrait *Giovanni Arnolfini and His Bride* (1434) in astonishingly precise detail. The painting is believed to celebrate the wedding of an Italian merchant, Giovanni Arnolfini, and many of its details refer to the sacred union of marriage.

GLITTERING GLASS

The English architect Robert Smythson was greatly influenced by Italian architectural ideas. His design for Hardwick Hall (completed 1597) in Derbyshire, England, included so many windows that it was described as "more glass than wall."

The Renaissance legacy

As RENAISSANCE HUMANISM spread across Europe during the 16th century, it gave people the freedom to look at the world in fresh ways, to express individual thoughts, and to question traditional views. And the achievements of the Renaissance went on to inspire and influence the Western world in the following century. Painters and sculptors were no longer regarded as craftsmen but as fine artists. Writers such as Shakespeare could use language with a new exuberance and beauty. Scientists such as Newton could examine how the universe functioned. The philosophers Blaise Pascal (1623–62) and René Descartes (1596–1650) could look rationally at the relationship between human beings and God.

PAINTING A LIFE
Over 40 years, the great Dutch painter Rembrandt van Rijn (1606–69) produced a series of self-portraits. These made an unflinchingly honest record of the artist's life, from youthful success, through loss and bankruptcy, to old age. The series embodies the humanist theme that each person's experience is unique and tells an individual story.

Rembrandt at age 23

Rembrandt at age 55

Cambridge University, England

CENTER OF LEARNING
Many Renaissance statesmen encouraged the spread of humanist learning. The famous Dutch scholar Erasmus was, for a time, professor of Greek at Cambridge University in England, which became a center of humanist teaching.

A NEW LITERATURE
The Spanish writer Miguel de Cervantes (1547–1616) created two immortal comic characters, the country gentleman Don Quixote, and his squire Sancho Panza. The best-selling adventures of Don Quixote not only made fun of Renaissance chivalry, but were also the model for a new kind of anti-heroic fiction.

Don Quixote's scrawny old horse, Rocinante

THE THEATRE
William Shakespeare (1564–1616) forged a fresh and dynamic kind of verse drama, often using earlier plays and romances as his sources. Many of his plays, such as *The Merchant of Venice* and *Romeo and Juliet*, were set in Renaissance Italy. Much of Shakespeare's greatest work was first performed at the Globe in London, an open-air theater built in 1599. This model shows the stage and surrounding galleries. In 1997, a working reconstruction of Shakespeare's Globe was completed near the original site.

In the painting, the king of France leans over the dying Leonardo – in reality he was not present at the deathbed

Side view of a replica of Newton's reflecting telescope

DEATH OF A GENIUS
Leonardo da Vinci died in May 1519 near Amboise in France, the guest of King Francis I. This romanticized picture of the scene was painted three centuries later by the French artist Jean Auguste Dominique Ingres. Leonardo's influence on art has been enormous, and many of the images he created – the *Mona Lisa*'s smile, Vitruvian man, the flying machine – are still familiar today.

THE ADVANCE OF SCIENCE
Sir Isaac Newton (1642–1727) was an English physicist and mathematician who carried on the revolutionary work of Galileo. He showed that the universe is held together by the force of gravity, and he also worked out important theories about light and motion.

Gallery, where richer spectators sat

Box, or gentleman's room

Balcony above the stage for musicians

The stage projected into the yard

Index

Acknowledgments

Dorling Kindersley would like to thank:
Alan Hills and Dora Thornton at the British Museum; the Museum of London; the Shakespeare Globe Trust; Signora Pelliconi at the Soprintendenza per i beni artistici e strorici; the Museo Horne; the Bargello in Florence (photographs used on concession by the Ministry of Beni Culturali ed Ambientali, Florence).

Art consultants: Alison Cole, Jill Dunkerton. **Map:** John Woodcock. **Modelmaker:** Peter Griffiths. **Jacket design:** Dean Price. **Additional photography:** Gary Ombler. **Index:** Chris Bernstein.

In-house assistance: Robert Graham, Bethany Dawn, Jill Bunyan, Anna Martin, Rose Hardy.

The publisher would like to thank the following for their kind permission to reproduce their photographs:
Key: a=above; b=below; c=center; l=left; r=right; t=top; Abbreviations: AKG: AKG London; BAL: Bridgeman Art Library, London; MEPL: Mary Evans Picture Library; SCA: Scala Firenze; V&A: Victoria and Albert Museum, London.

Jacket: Front: tcll Alan Hills; br Musee du Louvre, Paris; bl, detail AKG; clb *Equestrian Monument of Sir John Hawkwood* by Paolo Uccello, Duomo, Firenze/SCA; tl Musee du Louvre, Paris/Photographie Giraudon; c Museo della Scienza e della Tecnica, Milano/SCA; Inside front: tl, detail AKG; tr AKG; cra, detail *Figure Study for Battle of Cascina 1504,* by Michelangelo Buonarroti, British Museum; b Museo della Scienza e della Tecnica, Milano/SCA; Back: tcll Alan Hills; cra, detail AKG; tl Musee du Louvre, Paris/Photographie Giraudon; br Hulton Getty; bl, detail SCA; cl Biblioteca Nazionale, Firenze/SCA; Spine: detail AKG.

Page 9 p9: bl Bibliotheque Nationale, Paris/AKG; tr Cott Nero E II pt2 f.20v *The Expulsion of the Albigensians from Carcassonne: Catherist heretics of the 12th and 13th centuries,* from "The Chronicles of France, from Priam King of Troy until the crowning of Charles VI," (by the Boucicaut Master and Workshop, Chronicles of France, 1388 British Library, London)/BAL; br MEPL; **Pages 10-11** p10: bl

Frontispiece to Petrarch's Copy of Maurius Servius Honoratus's "Commentary on Virgil," 1340 by Simone Martini (1284-1344) Biblioteca Ambrosiana, Milan/BAL; tl Museo Pio-Clementino Vaticano/ SCA; p11: tr, detail *Primavera,* c.1478, (tempera on panel) by Sandro Botticelli (1444/5-1510) Galleria Degli Uffizi, Firenze/BAL; tl Museo dell' Opera Metropolitana, Siena/SCA; br Palazzo Vecchio, Firenze/SCA; **Pages 12-13** p12: br, detail *Portrait of Lionello d'Este* by Antonio Pisanello (1395-1455) Galleria dell'Accademia Carrara, Bergamo/BAL; tl SCA; bl, detail Pinacoteca di Brera Milano/SCA; p13: bl, detail *Federigo da Montefeltro, Duke of Urbino,* c.1465 (panel) by Piero della Francesca (c.1419/21-92) Galleria Degli Uffizi, Firenze/BAL; tr Museo Dell' Opera del Duomo, Firenze/SCA; **Pages 14-15** p14: r, detail *Portrait of Henry VIII* by Hans the Younger Holbein (1497/8-1543) Belvoir Castle, Leicestershire, UK/BAL; p15: l, detail AKG; r, detail Vatican Museum, Rome/AKG; tc *Portrait of Francis I on Horseback,* c.1540 by Francois Clouet (c.1510-72) Galleria degli Uffizi, Firenze/BAL; tr Accademia Venezia/SCA; **Pages 16-17** p16: bl National Maritime Museum; br MEPL; tr MEPL; p17: tl Alan Hills; **Pages 18-19** p18: tl *Equestrian Monument of Sir John Hawkwood* (fresco) by Paolo Uccello (1397-1475) Duomo, Firenze/BAL; c *Henry VIII (1491-1547)* and *Parliament in 1523* (engraving) by English School (16th century) Private Collection/AKG; p19: tl Museo di San Marco, Firenze/AKG; tl *Portrait of Niccolo Machiavelli (1469-1527)* by Santi di Tito (1536-1603) Palazzo Vecchio, Firenze/BAL; c MEPL; **Pages 20-21** p20: l SCA; br SCA; p21: b, detail *Adoration of the Magi* by Sandro Botticelli (1444/5-1510) Galleria Degli Uffizi, Firenze/BAL; tr *Portrait Bust of Lorenzo de' Medici* by Andrea del Verrocchio (1435-88) Palazzo Medici-Riccardi, Firenze/BAL; tc SCA; **Pages 22-23** p22: bc AKG; br, detail *Libyan Sibyl* by Michelangelo Buonarroti (1475-1564) Vatican Museums and Galleries, Rome/AKG; c Louvre, Paris/ET Archive; **Pages 26-27** p26: br *The Lady with the Ermine* (Cecilia Gallerani) by Leonardo da Vinci (1452-1519) Czartorisky Museum, Krakow/AKG; p27: tr *Ginevra dei Benci* (Reverse) © 1999 Board of Trustees, National Gallery of Art, Washington; r Musee, Paris/ET AKG; **Pages 28-29** p28: tl View of the main altar (photo) San Miniato Al Monte, Firenze/BAL; br National Gallery, London; p29: br Fr 12420 f.86 *The Story of Thamyris,* from 'De Claris Mulieribus' "Works of Giovanni Boccaccio" (1313-75) Bibliotheque Nationale, Paris/BAL; tl National Gallery, London; cb

gemstones Natural History Museum **Pages 30-31** p30: tl detail Fort Belvedere and the Pitti Palace from a series of lunettes depicting views of the Medici Villas, 1599 by Giusto Utens (fl.1599-1609) Museo di Firenze Com'era, Firenze/BAL; cl Royal Collection Enterprises (The Royal Collection ©1999 Her Majesty Queen Elizabeth II); 30-31 b SCA; p31: tl *The Month of October,* c.1400 (fresco) by Italian School (15th Century) Castello del Buonconsiglio, Trent/BAL; tr Royal Collection Enterprises (The Royal Collection ©1999 Her Majesty Queen Elizabeth II); cr Royal Collection Enterprises (The Royal Collection ©1999 Her Majesty Queen Elizabeth II); **Pages 32-33** p32: bc Warburg Institute (University of London); p33: br AKG; **Pages 34-35** p34: tl Szepmueveszeti Muzeum, Budapest AKG; cl *Study for the Battle of Anghiari,* 1504-5 (pen & ink) by Leonardo da Vinci (1452-1519) Galleria dell' Accademia, Venice/BAL; bl Daspet; cr Mus. du Louvre, Paris/ Photographie Giraudon; p35: cl Museo Nazionale del Bargello, Firenze/AKG; tr *Figure Study for Battle of Cascina 1504,* pen, brush, brown and grey ink (W.6 recto) by Michelangelo Buonarroti (1475-1564) British Museum, London/BAL; tl *The Battle of Cascina,* after Michelangelo (1475-1564) by Antonio da Sangallo, the elder (1455-1534) Holkham Hall, Norfolk/BAL; clb *The Sacrifice of Isaac,* bronze competition relief for the Baptistry Doors, Firenze, 1401-2 by Filippo Brunelleschi (1377-1446) Museo Nazionale del Bargello, Firenze/BAL; **Pages 36-37** p36: tl, detail *Warrior with Groom (Il Gattamelata)* by Giorgione (Giorgio da Castelfranco) (1476/8-1510) Galleria Degli Ufffizi, Firenze/BAL; bl, detail British Museum, London; bl *Portrait of a Child* by Sofonisba Anguissola (1527-1625) The Trustees of Weston Park Foundation/BAL; r, detail *Portrait of Dona Margarita de Cardona, wife of Count Adam of Dietrichstein* (oil on canvas) by Titian follower Roudnice Lobkowicz Coll., Nelahozeves Castle, Czech Republic /BAL; **Pages 38-39** p38: bl Vinci Tourist Office; p39: crb V&A; **Pages 42-43** p42: bc Image Select; bl, detail Oeffentliche Kunstsammlung Basel, Kunstmuseum; r The Wellcome Trust (Wellcome Institute Library, London); p43: tl Hunter 364 (TOP V14 f.59) *John Bannister delivering an anatomy lesson* Glasgow University Library/BAL; bc Royal Collection Enterprises (The Royal Collection ©1999 Her Majesty Queen Elizabeth II); br Royal Collection Enterprises (The Royal Collection ©1999 Her Majesty Queen Elizabeth II), bl

gemstones Natural History Museum; **Pages 44-45** p44: c Hulton Getty; bl Museo della Scienza e della Tecnica, Milano/SCA; 44-45 t Museo della Scienza e della Tecnica, Milano/SCA; p45: br MEPL; **Pages 46-47** p46: cr MEPL (Explorer Archives); tl Hulton Getty; bl, detail SCA; br Science Photo Library; p47: tl MEPL; tr Hulton Getty; bl Biblioteca Nazionale, Firenze/SCA; c Museo della Scienza, Firenze/SCA; c Science Photo Library; **Pages 48-49** p48: b Museo Nazionale della Scienza e della Tecnica "Leonardo da Vinci"; ac Science & Society Picture Library; cr Science & Society Picture Library ; p49: c, detail *Head of a Warrior* (drawing) by Leonardo da Vinci (1452-1519) British Museum, London/BAL; bl and ac Wallace Collection, London; **Pages 50-51** p50: cra Biblioteca Laurenziana, Firenze/SCA; bc Museum of London; tc both Science Museum, London p51: tr MEPL; **Pages 52-53** p52: l Add 42130 f.182v Text, and grotesque - the hybrid monster composed of animal and human parts, begun prior to 1340 for Sir Geoffrey Luttrell (1276-1345), Latin, Luttrell Psalter, (14th century); British Library, London/BAL; c British Library br MEPL; tr MEPL; p53: t Add 42130 f.182v Text, and grotesque - the hybrid monster composed of animal and human parts, begun prior to 1340 for Sir Geoffrey Luttrell (1276-1345), Latin, Luttrell Psalter, (14th century); British Library, London/BAL; c St Bride Printing Library; **Pages 54-55** p54: tl MEPL; Kunsthistorisches Museum ; cl Lebrecht Collection; bl, detail SCA p55: cr, detail AKG; br *The Stock Market;* **Pages 56-57** p58: cl *Adam* by Albrecht Durer (1471-1528) Prado, Madrid/BAL; br *Charon Crossing the River Styx* by Joachim Patenier or Patinir (1487-1524) Prado, Madrid/BAL; c *Eve* by Albrecht Durer (1471-1528) Prado, Madrid/BAL; cr *Hunters in the Snow - February 1565* by Pieter Brueghel the Elder (c.1515-69) Kunsthistorisches Museum, Vienna/BAL; tr MEPL; p59: tr AKG; bl National Gallery, London/AKG; tl *Portrait of Deiderius Erasmus (1466-1536)* by Hans the Younger Holbein (1497/8-1543) Louvre, Paris/BAL; cr MEPL; br National Trust Photographic Library; **Pages 58-59** p56: tc, detail *Self Portrait, 1629* by Harmensz van Rijn Rembrandt (1606-69) Mauritshuis, The Hague, Netherlands/BAL; cra, detail *Self Portrait, 1661-62* by Harmensz van Rijn Rembrandt (1606-69) Kenwood House, London/BAL; tl MEPL; c Tony Stone Images (John Lawrence); p57: tl *Francis I Cradling the Dying Leonardo da Vinci, 1818* by Jean Auguste Dominique Ingres (1780-1867) Musee du Petit Palais, Paris/BAL; tr Science Museum.